# RESTACKING CAPS AND LOVING THE MONKEYS WHO TOOK THEM

Blunders, Conflicts, and Redemption in
the Early Journey of a Peddler of Soul Mending

Brad Bull, M.Div., Ph.D., LMFT

Jacket design by the author.*  Images were adapted from:

*Monkey Tavern* (undated)
David Teniers the Youngers (1610-1690)

*Jesus Among the Doctors* **
1506, Albrecht Dürer

*The Scream*
1893, Edvard Munch

*Adam and Eve in the Garden of Eden*
ca.1520-1525, The Elder Lucas Cranach

*Penitent St. Jerome*
ca. 1620s, Georges de La Tour

*The Return of the Prodigal Son*
1665, Rijn Van Rembrandt

*You can contact the author via e-mail at bradleywbull@gmail.com .

**Note that the image from *The Scream* was superimposed over the image of Christ in *Jesus Among the Doctors*. Since this is an inductive book, I'll let you ponder why I did that and why all but one of the pictures are askew.

Parson's Porch Books

*Restacking Caps and Loving the Monkeys Who Took Them*

Copyright © 2012 by Bradley W. Bull

ISBN: 978-1-936912-65-0    Softcover

All rights reserved. No part of this book may be reproduced or transmitted in any form or by any means, electronic or mechanical, including photocopying, recording, or by any information storage and retrieval system, without permission in writing from the publisher.
This book was printed in the United States of America.

To order additional copies of this book, contact:

Parson's Porch Books
1-423-475-7308
www.parsonsporchbooks.com

# DEDICATION

Throughout my life, I have been greatly aided by ministers, counselors, doctors, and municipal sanitation workers. I dedicate this book to all of them.

I want to give special recognition to several of them. Rev. Steve Carter, my first mentor, helped me believe God could work in and through me. Dr. Bill Fletcher, my first counselor, helped me truly experience grace for the first time. Dr. Greg Glover brought both my children into the world through two difficult pregnancies and helped Connie and me through two miscarriages. Finally, I dedicate this book to those persons who, on Fridays— sometime between when I leave for work and when I get home— haul away my garbage that I have deposited by the road in a locked can that keeps storms and varmints from inflicting my trash on my neighbors.

# ACKNOWLEDGMENTS

Thanks to all who have shared their lives and stories with me and have given me grace when I bungled my assistance to them. Thanks to my parents, Dr. Bernard and Barbara Bull for giving me life and love. Thanks to my wife, Dr. Connie Cruze Bull, for helping re-stack my caps, and to my children, Delyn and John-Clarke, for reminding me to stop and play. Thanks to Jeff Dan Marion, my college creative writing professor, for laughing and crying. I deeply appreciate Carol McDonald and Jo Helen Stephenson for offering invaluable assistance with early drafts of this book. I asked various seminary and college professors to review a late manuscript; I appreciate all of them, from Dr. Harold Bryson's strong affirmation, to the candor of one who despised the very existence of this book with its frank discussion of sexual temptation, liberal use of contractions and introspective style. In response to this person's rather harsh criticism, but without telling the next reviewer about it, I asked our family friend and former seminary classmate Lea Alexander for a review. She provided additional meticulous technical feedback but also affirmation. When I told her about the negative review, she defended producing such a candid book, saying: "Much pain is caused by our lack of honestly facing our weaknesses. ... I was just thrown into my first ministry internship with no guidance; I wish I had had a book like this early in my career." I then asked Jody Baker, a recent college graduate exemplifying profound faith, integrity, and scholarship to perform a final reading of the manuscripts. She strongly affirmed the manner in which sensitive issues are address in this book. Finally, I want to express thanks for the preparation provided by my Clinical Pastoral Education supervisors and Sara Cawood, my family therapy trainer, all of whom challenged me and were patient with me even when I hated their meddling guts. therapy trainer, all of whom challenged me and were patient with me even when I hated their meddling guts.

# PREFACE

One of our family's favorite books to read aloud is the classic children's tale, *Caps for Sale*, by Esphyr Slobodkina. I loved the story when I was a child. Now I love holding my children in my lap as I read the story with an affected Slavic accent.

In the story, a cap salesman carries his wares on his head. One day, having little success at sales, the peddler sits down under a tree to take a nap. When he awakens he discovers that monkeys have absconded with his caps and are teasing him with them from up in the tree under which the peddler had slept. He stomps his foot and says, "You monkeys, you. Give me back my caps!"

Caps. Hats. "Wearing many hats" is an idiom for having many jobs. I wrote this book at the midpoint of a career in which I have worn many caps. During seminary I served two different churches as a youth minister; I also worked as aide at a psychiatric hospital, and I was a reporter for a denominational state news journal. When I left seminary, I spent one year as a chaplain in an intensive Clinical Pastoral Education hospital residency. After my residency, I became associate pastor for youth and young adults at a church where I served for eight years. During that time, I also entered an internship at a counseling center where I became a licensed marriage and family therapist. I also began taking classes toward a Ph.D. in human ecology, majoring in child and family studies with a cognate in counseling. After eight years, I left the church to go to school full time and finish that degree. While working full time on my courses and dissertation, I served as a graduate teaching assistant at the university and as an interim contemporary preacher at a church. After finishing my degree, I took a position as a family therapist at a non-denominational faith-based counseling center. I left that to take a position teaching undergraduate psychology and then on to graduate counseling. So, I have worn a lot of hats: chaplain, church minister, writer, teacher, counselor. Many times these roles have overlapped. But a common denominator in wearing all these hats is that, like the peddler, my hats often have been threatened by monkeys—external to me and within myself—crises and conflicts that seemed to threaten either me, my job, my coworkers, my hospital patients, my congregation members, or my clients. But then there have been the times when, as with the peddler, the hats came drifting back down and, with relief, I stacked them and started over again.

When I was a child I used to watch a police drama on TV. At the beginning the narrator said, "The story you are about to hear is true. The names have been changed to protect the innocent." If it is important to protect the innocent in criminal cases, it is even more important to protect *everyone* in matters of such personal confidence as faith and health. In this book I have changed not only names but sometimes contexts and the subjects' genders. I often have created composite characters, while staying completely true to the essence of the events. In his book *People of the Lie*, psychiatrist Scott Peck says that if friends and colleagues reading the book think they know the people about whom he has written, they are mistaken. The same is true of this book. My wife has read all these stories and tried to guess the identities of the people involved. She has only guessed one correctly, and it was in a situation where I did not need to disguise the person's identity. So, to readers who may have been involved in my life and work, let me say, any similarity between persons in these stories and mutual acquaintances of ours is strictly coincidental. In point of fact, these stories are not about any individuals. Every story is about each of us. You and I are the angry, abusive, drug-abusing, promiscuous, arrogant, depressed, and injured church members, patients, clients, and coworkers. You and I also are the laughing, joyous, persistent, growing, humbled, and recovering sojourners, continuously endeavoring to re-stack our caps and continue on our way.

# PREPILOGUE

One of my reviewers said this book needed an epilogue, so I wrote one. Having written it, I think it contains one of the most important messages in the book, and I fear that people who don't make it to the end might not read it. Thus, I'm moving a portion of the epilogue from the traditional location. I figure if George Lucas could do a prequel with *Star Wars*, I can coin the neologism "prepilogue" and put my epilogue at the beginning of my own story of struggles, defeats, and victories.

I started writing this book in July 2005 just after finishing my dissertation and during the 1-year period I was looking for a job. (During the Christmas season of 2005, in the weeks after graduation, I worked as a seasonal driver-helper for UPS. I was the first Ph.D. driver-helper in the history of UPS in Knoxville, TN. But I made enough money to buy my children some Christmas presents.) In the winter of 2005-06, I sent the first five chapters of this book to a publisher who said, "We want to see the completed book of at least 12 chapters." I kicked into high gear, finished the other chapters and mailed the manuscript. At the same time I was offered a job teaching psychology at a small, private, sectarian college. The second week I was there, a thin envelope arrived from the publisher. I was heartbroken; I knew a thin envelope meant no contract. The letter said, "This is not the kind of material we currently are seeking." I thought, *You didn't know that after five chapters?*

Now I was completely swamped with my teaching load in my rookie year of teaching and did not resubmit the manuscript to anyone. Then after just one year at my new job, I was begged to come back and teach at my alma mater. Against the still, small voice telling me not to, but out of a sense of loyalty, I left a job I loved to go to a place I loved. After five years, and the year before I was eligible for tenure, my position was one of several eliminated in budget cuts. (The month after I lost my job, two reviews of this book came back to me from retired professors. One said, "[Our field] NEEDS this book." The other said I appeared obsessed with sex and that this book could lead to the loss of my job; he returned the manuscript without finishing it.) "Budget cuts" is the short version of the political forces that led to the loss of my job and does not capture the monkeys that temporarily stole my new cap, this time a mortar board.

But as I write this, I am in my third month at my new job at a new university. There are many wonderful things that have happened— not only in spite of losing my job but also *because* of what happened.

When I told my children that I had lost my job, I said that we would have to be even more frugal than usual. "We already don't have cable TV or fancy cars. But we may have to give up our cell phones and things like that." My then 10-year-old son said, "Dad, I don't have to buy those magnets I wanted. You can have my $5. Will that help?"

Earlier that day a colleague, upon hearing about my job, said through tears, "I wish my kids were affectionate to me like yours are to you. Where it matters most, you've got it. You don't have a job, but you have kids that love you. Nobody can take that away." The most important cap I wear, is the parent cap, and I apologize to my children for the times I have let my anger over other stolen caps knock my parent cap askew.

# CONTENTS

Chapter 1: The Bulldog     17

Chapter 2: A Better Bumper Sticker     32

Chapter 3: Yea, Though I Forget the Words to the 23rd Psalm     40

Chapter 4: The Godly's in the Detailing     52

Chapter 5: The Slings and Arrows of Contagious Misfortunes     59

Chapter 6: What You Goose On Earth Shall Be Goosed in Heaven     71

Chapter 7: Death, Proctologist Appointments, and Weddings     85

Chapter 8: Lock-ins are of Satan... Except When They're Not     98

Chapter 9: Thou Shalt Not "Play Tennis" but with Thine Own Partner     130

Chapter 10: Through the Perilous Fight     145

Chapter 11: Touching Stories     156

Chapter 12: Congruence     172

Chapter 13: Dealing with Cleavage     197

Chapter 14: As Uno with Authoritatis     214

# CHAPTER 1

## The Bulldog

"Code 99, ICU 16. Code 99, ICU 16. Code 99, ICU 16."

It was the last room on the left of the intensive care unit's north wing. If The Unit were a metronome, the weight on its pendulum had just been shoved to the bottom, the new tempo frantic but controlled. "A code is controlled chaos," my supervisor had instructed our class of three intern chaplains.

In our hospital, "Code 99" referred to a patient going into cardiac or respiratory arrest. Another hospital where I had worked used "Code Blue," possibly referring to the pallor of skin not getting oxygen. But in a time just before easy text messaging, our hospital used numeric codes that were easy to transmit to digital pagers. So when a patient coded, a red button at the head of the patient's bed was pressed (unless the patient was hooked up to a monitor, in which case the alarm was sent automatically). The alarm went straight to the switchboard desk, where two operators would immediately end any calls they were handling. One would begin sending electronic pages to the code team: the respective doctors, therapists, technicians, and the on-call chaplain. At night, the operators were supposed to activate the pager of the on-call chaplain— who had to be within 20 minutes of the hospital. If we lived farther than 20 minutes, we could stay in the on-call room across the street in a hotel owned by the hospital. I lived just at the edge of the 20-minute margin. So I stayed in the on-call room, depending on my mood— like being in the mood to have access to cable TV and my wife being in the mood to stay at the hospital with me, adding 20 minutes to her commute to work. Wherever I was, I preferred to get a page first as opposed to a telephone call. But the operators seemed to take sadistic pleasure in calling chaplains in order to hear our groggy voices before we had a chance to be fully awake. In their defense, the operators would sometimes tell us that there was no family present at the hospital and we really weren't needed. In those cases we could turn over and go back to sleep without having to respond to the page. The other operator would call over the hospital public address system, repeating the code and its location three times in the understated tone reminiscent of the NASA announcer who, when the space shuttle Challenger exploded during liftoff, with the poise of an easy-listening radio DJ said, "Obviously a major malfunction."

    I was only a few months into my residency, and this was my first code in the intensive care unit. ICU was not one of my assigned areas, but I was the on-call chaplain, and that meant I responded to any code. The first six months of my one-year residency I was assigned to geriatric psych, coronary care, and the radiation treatment waiting area. The second half of the year I rotated from geriatric to adult psych and from radiation waiting to the emergency room, but I worked in coronary care, including the Coronary Care Unit and its waiting room, all year. Working in coronary care, I had already seen my share of codes. But when I opened the stout wooden door to The Unit, some indescribable nature of the flurry of activity at the opposite end of the corridor already gave this one a different feel. Maybe it was just the fact that it was new geographical terrain for me.

    As I strode down the hall, I heard once again the words of my supervisor echoing through my head. "A code is controlled chaos. Everyone has an assigned task. Orders are being barked. In the midst of such chaos, people can be aided by an icon of peace. Or as *my* supervisor used to say to *me*, 'Don't just do something; stand there!'"

I assumed a position across the hall from the door to Bed 16. I stood with my back to the wall, my hands interlinked in front of me. I was the one in the suit and tie. The folks in scrubs were scrambling here and there. Even the people standing in one position were moving: a male orderly on the left side of the bed was administering compressions on the chest of a slightly obese, elderly, white male, who looked to be an octogenarian; a doctor with reading glasses perched on his nose was preparing a tube— he slid it in the patient's side, and blood and some other body fluid erupted. Then I noticed a petite brunette female— in the blue smock of a respiratory therapist— was standing by the bank of monitors in the back right corner— unusually still, pallid.

From my left, I heard the main door I had just entered moments earlier slam open. A short, stocky doctor marched toward me double time, walking like a cartoon bulldog with his elbows flared out and his fists, lurching by his waist, matching the staccato of his feet. I had the sense that the cavalry had not arrived, but George Patton had. He pivoted into the door opening and stomped to a wide-stanced stop, left fist on hip, right hand raised holding up two fingers. "TWO TIMES IN THREE WEEKS! WHAT THE HELL ARE YOU PEOPLE DOING TO MY PATIENTS? I'M GOING TO LOSE MY SURGICAL LICENSE!!!"

The doctor on the right side of the bed glanced impassively over his glasses at The Bulldog. But just beneath those impassive eyes, I seemed to see the slightest hint of *"Shut up and help, you . . ."* ninny? Arrogant . . . ? What was that doctor thinking about his colleague, I wondered. Already I was struck that The Bulldog's primary concern seemed to be over losing his license rather than his patient. We were a private sectarian hospital. As the profanity continued to ricochet around the room, I couldn't help but think, *I bet this won't be part of the hospital president's report at the state Baptist convention this year.*

"WHAT HAPPENED?" he bellowed, now moving toward the left side of the bed to busy himself watching the now sweating orderly performing compressions.

The respiratory therapist spoke up over the din. "I was giving him a treatment... "

"I DON'T WANT YOU PEOPLE TOUCHING ANY MORE OF MY PATIENTS. I CAN'T KEEP LOSING PATIENTS THREE DAYS POST-OP!"

The respiratory therapist fled the room and, crossing the threshold back into the hall where I was still standing like a Secret Service agent, erupted into tears. I spotted a box of tissues on the nurses' station desk and gestured to the clerk who handed her one.

She sobbed, "I was just giving him a treatment - - I was following procedure - - I had just adjusted a tube - - and he coded!" She continued on, repeating to the clerk and me the steps she had taken.

The entrance door at the far end of the hall opened again. It was The Shy-Bearded-Man-in-a-Blue-Lab-Coat. He came to a stop before us. His concerned but sterile gaze uttered a voiceless, "What happened?" The therapist reiterated her account to her supervisor.

Meanwhile, inside the room, The Bulldog had pronounced the patient dead and called off the code. He strode out of the room headed toward the ICU entrance  To my shock, the respiratory therapy supervisor said, "Excuse me, Dr. ... ."

*BAD idea*, I thought. *He's irate, and this is no time for a debriefing.*

The Bulldog whipped around. The Shy-Bearded-Man-in-a-Blue-Lab-Coat said, "I'd like to talk about what happened."

"I'LL TELL YOU WHAT HAPPENED . . .!"

In the ensuing exchange, the respiratory therapist was standing to my right, her supervisor was just in front of her to her right, and the doctor was to my left, so that I must have looked like someone watching a tennis match.

"I HAD JUST TOLD HIS FAMILY HE WAS OK AND THEY COULD GO HOME! AND TWO HOURS LATER, HE'S DEAD!"

The supervisor started to say something about protocol; The Bulldog interrupted. The therapist started to say something about protocol; The Bulldog interrupted. The supervisor started to . . . . The Bulldog interrupted. The therapist tried to explain
that . . . .

The Bulldog stuck his finger just inches from the therapist's face and poked it at her face with each of his words. "YOU KILLED MY PATIENT."

That was it. As the therapist melted into sobs I stepped between them. I looked down at the doctor with my hands linked at my waist and whispered, "Doc, this woman is going through hell. I know you are, too." Then I lifted my palms toward him and with my eyes said, "Back off."

He whirled around, marched three steps, then whipped back around and yelled, "I AM ONLY CONCERNED ABOUT THE LIVES OF MY PATIENTS!" Then he pointed at the supervisor, and said, "THAT'S WHAT YOU'RE SUPPOSED TO BE CONCERNED ABOUT," at the therapist, "THAT'S WHAT YOU'RE SUPPOSED TO BE CONCERNED ABOUT," and finally at me, "AND THAT'S WHAT *YOU'RE* SUPPOSED TO BE CONCERNED ABOUT!" With that he turned and strode out of the unit.

I turned and gave the supervisor a glance that said, "The nerve of that guy." I wanted to offer the same to the therapist, but with her head down, sobbing, no glance, no matter how compassionate, would be able to console her. Out of the corner of my eye and with my ears, I could tell that the mournful solemnity of a lost battle had fallen over the room as nurses and orderlies began the process of cleaning up in the midst of the haunting presence of the hallowed corpse of a man who was born prior to World War I, had endured the Depression and World War II and raised a family of children and grandchildren who would, any moment now, arrive back home to bad news.

Given the scene going on just a few feet away, I thought it might be helpful to get some distance between the therapist and the room. There was another desk about half-way down the hall. "Let's go down to the other desk," I directed. She willingly followed. I surreptitiously gestured for the clerk to bring her a cup of coffee. Arriving at the other desk, a female nurse began consoling the therapist with hushed disparaging remarks about The Bulldog and that, of course, she had done what she was supposed to do. The clerk handed the therapist the cup of coffee. She cradled it in her trembling hands and sipped it like breaths of air. The supervisor asked me what I had said to the doctor. I told him.

Suddenly it struck me that moving to the desk was not far enough removed. I suggested that we move to the respiratory therapy office. The nurse hugged the therapist, and the other three of us went to another floor of the hospital to an office I had never been to before.

The therapist finally sat down. She began telling the supervisor she was going to quit. She thanked me for what I had done. After a few minutes, the head of respiratory therapy walked in the office. I knew him only as Muscular-Freud-In-A-Starched-Tight-White-Shirt-And-Tie, and he looked wide-eyed with concern and questions. The story was recounted by the therapist, then by the supervisor. ". . . Then the chaplain stepped between them and told Dr. [Machiavelli] he needed to back off.

Muscular-Freud-In-A-Starched-Tight-White-Shirt-And-Tie shot me a look. "You said that to a doctor?" I hadn't said those words exactly, but that had been my clear message. "Yes." Emphatically, the head of respiratory therapy said, "You need to go to your supervisor right now and tell him."

My confidence melted into abject fear. I didn't fear the doctor. But I was terrified of my supervisors. I had been since my second full day on the job. On my first full day, the head of our department—a man with the kind-hearted face of a beloved uncle but the battle-hardened experience of a combat chaplain in Vietnam—conceded during rounds (morning briefing) that he had forgotten to prepare a sermon for chapel that day. I had volunteered that I had a sermon ready. The department head initially seemed excited. "Really!? Well, no. I'll do it. But thanks." The next day during Interpersonal Relations (IPR)—a dialog intended to confront interns' fears and neuroses—the issue was raised about my previous day's attempt at "rescuing." Under the heat of examination, I lied. "You all thought I was seriously offering to preach? I was just kidding." Then, I paid a heavy price for lying, for not just owning that my understanding of my "do unto others" rearing was now being labeled pathological. The head of pastoral care looked at me and scowled, "You were kidding? You sure looked serious to me. Boy, I'm not going to be able to trust you." I looked at my supervisor, I could tell he knew I had lied about kidding. The next week I was on the floor visiting patients when I was paged over the intercom to call an extension I didn't recognize. "Where are you?" my supervisor barked. I told him. "Check your calendar," he said and hung up. Immediately I realized I was AWOL from our weekly IPR meeting and that I would accurately be labeled as "avoidant," having forgotten to go to the meeting where I had been raked over the coals the week before. Now, based on my understanding of the head of respiratory therapy, I was going to be accused of insubordination or—worse—rescuing.

I went to the pastoral care office. Both my supervisor and the department head were gone for the day. Until late in the evening I tried calling them at home to no avail. The next morning at the end of rounds, I exercised my right for a "called IPR" session. The pastoral counselor, the oncology chaplain, and the secretary went about their morning duties, and my two supervisors, my two fellow residents, and I went into the office of my immediate supervisor, the director of Clinical Pastoral Education (CPE).

We sat in a circle. The CPE director had a sly grin on his face. What was that about? The Department head had a twinkle in his eye. I feared their mood would soon change.

"Something happened in ICU yesterday. Bill [the head of respiratory therapy] told me I needed to talk to you all immediately, but you were gone. I tried to call you last night but didn't get you. I don't think I did the wrong thing, but if I did, I'll take my lashes and go on." I told the story.

The looks on my supervisors' faces did not change. They didn't appear to be growing angry. What was going on? I ended the story, sighed, and said, "There it is." I braced myself.

My department head, who had been leaning over on his chair's arm rest with his chin on his fist, sat up and smiled toward my CPE director who was sitting in his "halo position" with hands behind his head, rocked backed toward his desk. Then he looked at me with utter paternal (but not patronizing) affirmation.

"Brad, I got here at 6:00 this morning. I've been all over this hospital. [Dramatic Pause.] Let me tell you something, young man. You are one popular guy in this hospital. *Everybody* is talking about the chaplain who stood up to Dr. [Doe]. When I heard about it, I went and talked to Bill. He was not mad at you. He only told you to see us in order to CYA." ("CYA?" I had never heard that expression, but, given the context, it only took me a few split seconds to figure out what part of me was afraid of being kicked and needed to be covered.) "Bill said he has never been prouder of an employee in this hospital. He said one of his employees was being abused and you very appropriately and bravely stepped in and stopped it." [Another dramatic pause. Eyebrows raised.] "Now maybe you did it out of ignorance [of hospital politics], but you did it. Brad, I'd like to think that if it had been me up there I would have done the same thing. But I know I wouldn't have." He looked at my CPE supervisor who nodded in affirmation. Then back to me with a combat veteran's voice and words: "Son, what you did took balls. Good work." Then, with a dramatic pause he raised his eyebrows and said, "Don't ever do it again."

After a brief pause to let me know he was serious, he laughed at his own paradox, and my supervisor again grinned and raised his eyebrows, nodding his head in affirmation. He seemed proud of me, like the time I confronted him with my perception of his anger with me during rounds one morning. He had been telling a story about going to his son's high school football game. He said the other team nearly ran the opening kickoff back for a touchdown, but it had been saved by a great open-field tackle. I had interrupted and said, "And your son was the one who made the tackle." With excitement he had said, "Yeah!" The oncology chaplain said, "Wait a second, Brad, how did you know that?" "Why do you think he's telling the story?" I asked. Everyone laughed, and the oncology chaplain said, "Oh no, we're only two weeks into the year and the IPR mind games have already started!" But my supervisor had locked eyes with me in a blank stare. I thought I had embarrassed him and he was mad at me.

I asked him about it during personal supervision. He said, "No, I wasn't mad. I was in shock and envious. I thought, *gee, this guy's got more insight than I give him credit for.*" He then admitted that he was envious of my height of 6'2". "You walk into a room and you automatically have at least some respect. As a short, heavyset guy, I have to prove myself to everyone. So, I guess I was a little jealous that not only are you tall, you're insightful."

Then he looked at me with this look of pride that I had come far enough, under his tutelage, to confront him with it.

It was the same look he gave me on another occasion late in my residency when I virtually yelled at the department head, "You may think I'm a rescuer, but I think abandoning that woman just so I could go eat pizza and watch a movie would have been unprofessional, inhuman, and cruel!" We were debriefing an incident from a previous Friday night. I was on call. My two peers, our spouses and I were going to order a pizza and watch one of my favorite movies in the on-call room. An hour before we were to start I got a Code 99 page. A woman was now widowed. Like many of our coronary patients, she and her husband had been in the area on vacation. Like the incident in ICU, her family had just been told he was OK, and the adult children had begun their six-hour ride home. This was before cell phones were a ubiquitous commodity. I sat with her for four hours, waiting for her children to arrive back home so she could call them and tell them their father had died.

"She would have been OK," the department head said in debriefing. "You could have stayed for a while and then gone and had pizza and watched a movie with your peers and your wife. But you seem to have this need to rescue people."

When I unleashed my counterargument on the department head, my supervisor gazed at me with a glance subtle enough to say "good job" without being brazen enough to be insubordinate to our boss.

It was the same look I was getting from him now, having described my encounter with The Bulldog.

One of my peers who was assigned to ICU spoke up. "It seems to me that, in the midst of your story, the fact that has gotten lost is that a man died." I felt attacked. *I can't do it all*, I thought. The family was gone. What else was I supposed to do? "Yes," I responded, "that was part of my problem with the doctor's reaction. He seemed more concerned about his reputation than genuinely concerned about the patient."

One of my supervisors then asked me what I thought was underlying the doctor's behavior. I said I didn't know. He challenged me to think about it between now and the next IPR. The meeting was adjourned.

At the next IPR I presented a letter I had written to the doctor. I said I could not imagine the pressure of years of medical school and being responsible for people's lives. I said something poetic about writing the letter from a hospital balcony overlooking the river; that just on the other side of the walls from that peaceful river, so much chaos and conflict had erupted in the ICU, and I hoped that conflict would be brought to peaceful resolution.

My supervisor said he didn't like the letter. I had given away all my power by setting the doctor on a pedestal. "You went through four years of seminary. You have the responsibility of caring for people's minds and spirits. Why subordinate that to the doctor's training and responsibility? If you give the doctors your power, they will take it. That's why when we're talking one-on-one I call them by their first names. I have a professional degree just like them. If they call me by my first name, I call them by theirs." He paused, then went on. "What if I told you I was at a Christmas party one time where Dr. [Machiavelli] was drunk while being the surgeon on call? What if I told you that he went through a bitter divorce and is estranged from his family? I was standing in the foyer at church one day and he pointed at his son and said, 'I didn't know he came to church here.' Sure he's got a lot of responsibility. So do all the doctors. So could it be that he's just a . . . ?" (I don't remember my supervisor's exact words at this point. But I suspect he likened the doctor's behavior to that of a certain stubborn domesticated farm animal.)

The same peer who had seemed to question my handling of the ICU incident spoke up. "Well, I like your letter." It was a bold move. He was going against the supervisor. "I think you pour your heart out and model good behavior to him."

"So what are you going to do?" my other peer asked.

I thought for a moment. "I'm going to send it," I said. "I don't think it matters if I give him my power. I think I have to do the right thing whether he does or not, and I am genuinely concerned about him."

A few days later, after allowing time for him to receive and digest the letter, I confidently stepped off the elevator and approached his suite in the office tower. I was anticipating him sheepishly admitting he had been out of line and apologizing for his behavior.

He barreled out the foyer door just as I was about to open it. "Hi, Dr. [Doe]. I was just coming to see you," I said, extending my hand as I matched his pace, heeling him like a puppy. Extending his hand, he looked at me for a brief moment, finally recognized me, and said, "Oh, yes, I got your letter. Thank you. Yeah, as far as what happened the other day, sometimes you have to do things like that to keep folks on their toes." *To keep folks on their toes!?* I thought. My fantasy of reporting to my supervisor The Bulldog's conversion evaporated. *You shattered a person's confidence in a way that will make her timid and less able to care most effectively for her patients.*

In my mind I heard my father telling a story about my cutting my finger on a metal storm door when I was a toddler. At the emergency room, I was wailing at the top of my lungs. The doctor had come in to stitch me up. He held out his hands for a nurse to don his rubber gloves. She did so, but not to his satisfaction. The bridges between the gloves' fingers had not nestled all the way down to the bridges between his fingers. The doctor had begun shouting profanities, asking the nurse where she had gone to nursing school. "Here you were hurt and screaming and the doctor was throwing a fit over his gloves. I had words with him later." Suddenly I realized the part of my background that had informed my intervention in ICU.

As we walked down the hall, I smiled insincerely at the doctor. During the code, I had seen the other doctor look over his glasses. I wasn't sure what words were going through his mind about his colleague, but I knew what word was going through mine, and it wasn't the technical term The Bulldog had learned in gross anatomy.

I'm writing this about a dozen years after the events happened. It occurs to me now that, in confronting Dr. Machiavelli, while I was genuinely concerned about him, his staff, and patients, I came to be most excited about the possibility of one-upping my supervisor by attempting to convince the doctor of the error of his ways. I condemned the doctor for being more concerned about his reputation than the well-being of his patients. But once I felt like I had failed at correcting the doctor, once I failed at putting a notch in my belt, I wrote him off. I had forgotten about another lesson my father taught me: "People need love most when they deserve it least."

But when does providing care cross the threshold to inappropriate rescuing? If working in a hospital taught me anything, it was the challenge of defining thresholds.

At what point is one patient more serious than another and should be treated first? At what point is a pastoral visit too long? At what point is the quality of pastoral care more important than the number of patients visited? (Visit 98% and someone isn't being truly heard; visit 40% and some administrator who appropriates budgets but doesn't know indigestion from a hole in a patient's *ground of being* wonders what you're doing with your time.) At what point does showing concern to a suicidal patient provide him or her attention that reinforces their desire to make an attempt in order to return to the hospital? St. Augustine reportedly said, "Sometimes cruelty is the kindest love of all." But when does tough love become callousness? At what point is the patient beyond resuscitation and the code should be called? At what point does assisting someone cross the line and patronizingly foster dependency?

Of all these thresholds, my toughest struggle as a chaplain, which continues to bulldog me as a minister, parent, and human citizen is this: on the one hand, at what point does rescuing become patronizingly unhealthy, or, on the other hand, when does a failure to act constitute apathy or cowardice?

It's tempting to offer an answer. But maybe the reader needs to wrestle with that question.

**Question for Reflection**

At what point does rescuing become patronizingly unhealthy, or, on the other hand, when does a failure to act constitute apathy or cowardice?

# CHAPTER 2

## A Better Bumper Sticker

The large elderly woman was in the floor near the bathroom door in her room. She was virtually naked, her hospital gown down around her waist. Standing across the hall I could smell the feces. Her bowels had released when she had what would be her last heart attack. But for now the crash team was working feverishly to resuscitate her.

Sarcastic-Looking-Hippie-Doctor arrived. He looked like a nerdy version of Buffalo Bill but with a perpetual "You are so beneath me" look on his face. After several minutes of flat line, he called off the code.

The crash team began cleaning the room. The doctor was filling out paperwork. The floor's head nurse, like a child playing mother-may-I, addressed him. "Dr. Smithers? I was wondering if we could put her in her bed . . . so she could have some dignity."

The doctor snorted a baffled smile.

The nurse's caution melted instantly into full steam, teeth gritted. "DON'T YOU *DARE* LAUGH AT ME FOR THAT!" She even pointed her finger. I was in awe of this woman. But the doctor, with no change in facial expression whatsoever, patronizingly said "OK." He said it like he had just agreed to accept two five-dollar bills rather than one ten-dollar bill.

You never know where an experience will be applied in your life. After writing the above passage, I thought, *Well, that was short.* But that wasn't the end of the story. Some five years later, recounting that story to a group of teenagers would trigger a chain of events resulting in a teenage girl being removed from the home of her sexually abusive father. As I write this, even I am struck by how remote these connections seem.

The year after finishing my internship as a chaplain, I began another internship in pursuit of licensure as a marriage and family therapist. One day my supervisor was leading a didactic on suicide. She pointed out that many males commit suicide by gunshot or hanging. Females tend to take sleeping pills. "I call it the Sleeping Beauty Effect," Sara said. "Teenage girls have this fantasy of being found sleeping peacefully. They romanticize suicide."

This assertion echoed the words of Dr. Wade Rowatt, my seminary professor in a course entitled *Families in Crisis*. During a unit on suicide, Dr. Rowatt said, "Hollywood all too often romanticizes suicide. But unlike when *Thelma and Louise* drive their car over the cliff, suicide does not happen in slow motion to a soundtrack."

"To the contrary," Sara had continued, "suicide is anything but beautiful." "Whenever I'm talking to teenagers I try to debunk their idealizations of suicide by painting a picture as graphic and unromantic as possible, even if I overstate it. I talk about how people's bowels and bladders release when they die. So it is the ultimate in gross, not beauty."

I had seen it happen. It was easy to be convincing.

My youth group was in rare rapt attention. The night before, I had seen the movie *Romeo and Juliet*, starring Leonardo DiCaprio, and I was extemporizing during Sunday school announcements, using my position as associate pastor for a bully pulpit. When I said I had seen the movie, a chorus of "Oh I loved that movie" had lilted out from various members of the assembly whose cups o'erflowed with hormones. Using a classic ploy, I lured them into my web with comments of what I genuinely enjoyed about the film.

Then, offhandedly, I remarked, "So, it was *almost* a good movie."

"*Almost?!*" someone protested. "It was a *great* movie. What do you mean *almost?*"

"I thought the ending was very dangerous."

"*Dangerous*? What do you mean?"

"Have any of you ever seen someone stab themselves through the heart?" I asked.

My question was met with a room full of blank stares.

"Anybody?" I repeated. No one said yes.

"I bet if someone stabs themselves in the heart, there would be a lot of blood. But when the camera angle shifted to overhead and began panning back, you see Juliet lying beautifully there beside her Romeo. There's barely a hint of blood. They made it look like this was some beautiful thing. I don't think the closing soliloquy about tragedy overcame the visual impact that the death of Romeo and Juliet was a thing of beauty. I think if viewers were having a hard time and were contemplating suicide, the movie might make them think suicide would be a beautiful escape from their problems."

I began following Sara's advice and attempted to offer an alternative reality to the "Sleeping Beauty Syndrome." I graphically told the story about the woman in the hospital. As I looked around the room I happened to notice that one of the usually chipper 14-year-old females had a wide-eyed look of someone who felt . . . scared? . . . guilty? I checked for similar expressions on the faces of others. She was the only one who looked . . . convicted? I made a mental note to make a discreet follow-up with her after Sunday school. I concluded with Dr. Rowatt's comment that suicide does not happen in slow motion to a lofty sound track. The young woman looked like she was about to start crying.

After Sunday school I asked to speak with her. She said she was very scared for a friend whom she thought was suicidal. She told me she didn't think her friend was in immediate danger though. I told her I had a cassette tape she could borrow, a tape about helping a friend who may be suicidal. She said she would come by my office after the evening worship service.

She did.

In the course of our conversation, she told me her friend was being sexually abused by her father. She provided enough details that I knew that (1) she was, indeed, not using "friend" as a euphemism for herself and (2) her friend was apparently being abused and was in grave danger.

In the course of our conversation, the young woman in my office, rather than saying "my friend," actually used the girl's name, "Jane." It was the name of her best friend, another 14-year-old young woman I had met when eating lunch at their school. She used the name so matter-of-factly and distinctly I thought she had done it on purpose. I asked a question in which I used Jane's name.

The young woman in my office went pale. The wide-eyed look of being "caught" returned to her face. "How did you know it was Jane?" she asked.

"You just said so."

The young woman erupted in tears. "Oh, God! Brad, YOU CAN'T TELL ANYONE!"

My mind reeled. A few moments before I had thought I was being asked to help report the situation. Now it was all too clear that was not the case; she was asking me not to report an alleged case of child abuse.

"You know I can't do that. Even if I only *suspect* someone is being abused, I am *legally* required to report it."

The young woman suddenly leapt from her chair, reached across my desk, picked up the phone and punched in a number.

Through sobs: "DAD! LET ME SPEAK TO MOM! . . . MOM! I JUST ACCIDENTLY TOLD BRAD ABOUT *JANE*. HE SAYS HE HAS TO REPORT IT. CAN YOU COME DOWN HERE?"

My heart locked. This mother and I had had a roller-coaster relationship. Of late, I had been the object of what seemed like an inordinate degree of anger. (We would eventually have a very productive conversation in which we both owned and amended the manner in which we each were bringing anger with others into our relationship. She had been abused by a series of males, of whom I was a reminder, and she reminded me of someone with whom I had had a combative relationship.) Now I found myself feeling shocked and scared: shocked that this mother apparently knew about the alleged abuse but was a confederate in keeping the secret and scared of her wrath.

Almost before the phone was hung up, the mother walked into my office. She looked like we had disturbed a nap, but she grinned with a sleepy forced calm.

For the next 30 minutes I tried simultaneously to comfort the teen, assuage the mom, avoid being defensive, and be open to being convinced that breaking the law might be the right thing to do. One of my many former mentors had once— with lowered voice— said, "Have I ever suspected abuse and not reported it? Yes. But I only did it when I knew beyond any doubt that reporting would do more harm than good and I was in a position of leverage to know if it happened again and that the family knew I would report it if it did. If I reported it prematurely I would lose my ability to help them." I wasn't sure I agreed with that, and, when I posed that scenario at a conference on abuse, the facilitator emphatically said it was never appropriate *not* to report suspected abuse.

So, here I was with a hurting girl and a defensive mom in my office, and here I sat with nearly four years of seminary training, a year of hospital chaplaincy, and a family therapy internship under my belt. This was where the proverbial [rubber] hit the [road].

After about 30 minutes of posturing with the mother, we decided to call the best friend. She was spending the night at her grandmother's house. Mom and daughter went to pick her up and bring her back to the church.

While they were gone, I prayed earnestly. OK, maybe I worried earnestly. The first sentence was an effort at spiritualizing myself and this story. I would like to think I prayed, but, honestly, I don't remember. (In similar circumstances I know I have called my wife and said, "I'll be home late. I can't say why. Just pray.") They left, and, seemingly not too long afterward, the trio entered my office.

The best friend smiled at me with a sleepy, sad smile. I remember feeling relieved that she looked relieved. She seemed aware of the ensuing pain, but happier that the secret was out and the pain of molestation might be coming to an end.

She confirmed that her father had been forcing her to have sex. She understood that I had to report the matter. I walked her through the possible consequences. Her mother might divorce her father. Her father might successfully deny the whole thing. She might end up taken from her family. Simultaneously, she lowered her eyelids, nodded, and wanly smiled.

The four of us prayed together. I do remember that, though I don't remember what I prayed. I probably prayed that God would give wisdom and guidance to all involved in intervening on Jane's behalf. Did I pray for her father? If so, what did I say?

They left. The girls with their tear-stained faces . . . but Jane still with a sleepy-eyed smile that seemed to connote apprehensive relief. The mother with a superficial smile that seemed to say, "I'm putting on a front to help keep the girls calm, but you're making a big mistake."

The next day I called the Department of Human Services.

A few weeks later the girl from the Sunday school class and her mother and father, approached me after a youth meeting. The mother smiled an affirming smile. "Brad, we want to tell you what happened as a result of our conversation a few weeks ago." I braced myself. The smile was a ploy. *Here comes the "I told you so."* "Because the situation got reported, the rest of the family is going to move [out of state]. Jane is going to continue to live with her grandmother, but because it got reported, she's going to get money for support from the state. So, even though sometimes things don't work out well, sometimes they do." With that she smiled a smile I could tell was genuine. We had a group hug.

But how did things turn out in the long run? I don't know. About a year later I ran into Jane in the lobby of a movie theater. We exchanged pleasantries as you do when one person is leaving a movie and another is going in. She *seemed* happy.

Whatever has happened in her life, many factors have contributed. I hope my action was one of the good ones. That is to say, I hope Jane has become a healthy, productive person, but if not, there were many other factors besides my action that influenced that outcome. The simple fact is, I don't *know* what happened in the long run, but what I do know is that I did what I felt was right even though I was pressured not to. And I'm always struck by how that chain of events began with an elderly woman dying on a hospital room floor in her own feces and was linked to two teenage girls in a church, one of the girls facing unspeakable torment. Some people die in excrement, some people are living in it. And in these contexts . . . ministry happens.

**Questions for Reflection**
1) I don't remember exactly what I prayed with the women that night in my office. I mention wondering if I prayed for the alleged molester. Remembering that a lot of "well intentioned prayers" have been hurtful, what would you have prayed?
2) What is the law regarding reporting abuse in the state where you serve?
3) The popular but crude bumper sticker "!@#$ Happens" implies that some things happen for no reason. What is my motive for connecting this sentiment with the statement "Ministry Happens"? Compare and contrast your understanding of these two statements.

# CHAPTER 3

## Yea, Though I Forget the Words to the 23$^{rd}$ Psalm...

"The family has been expecting this death for some time, so this shouldn't take long. I'll be back soon."

Rookie mistake. I had said these words to my wife as I walked out the door of our house on my way to the hospital. I was the on-call chaplain and had just been paged due to the death of a woman who spent her last three weeks on one of my assigned units. I had never seen her when she was conscious. But I had often spoken with her rotund, bedraggled husband and four daughters— all of whom sported black t-shirts featuring professional wrestlers, country singers, or deer hunting motifs.

The on-call chaplain was responsible for the whole hospital in the evenings and on weekends, so we often encountered total strangers in the midst of crises. But, as in the case I was now encountering for the first time, we also were called into situations with families we knew relatively well.

I thought I knew this family well. "Mamma" had been struggling for every breath for three weeks. By the time I got to the hospital, the family would have punctuated the goodbyes they had been saying for several days and likely would be walking out the door.

When I walked onto the unit, the nurse solemnly guided me to a room I had never entered. I heard the loud sobs of one person on the other side of the door. It turned out to be a disheveled catchall conference room, break room, and lunch cart and computer monitor storage room. The table and carts had been pushed back into a recessed alcove containing a sink, cabinets, and coffee supplies. The chairs were arranged in a loose-knit square around the perimeter of the room.

As the nurse pushed the door open and ushered me into the room, I first saw one of the four daughters sitting in a chair against the wall to my left. All of the daughters appeared to be in their late twenties to very early thirties; this was the youngest. She was sniffling quietly, head down, a soaked tissue wadded in her pudgy hands.

As the door swung wider I stepped into the room. I saw "Daddy," a glum flat stare on his face, sitting straight across from the door with the table and carts behind him in the alcove. His hairy belly peeked from beneath the tail of his t-shirt. His thinning, greasy hair was slicked straight back, a sharp widow's peak dividing a shiny forehead, with one clump of strands dangling beside his left eye.

To my left, the oldest daughter was standing in the corner drinking a cup of coffee. To my right, the second daughter was sitting in a chair against the wall, rocking and loudly sobbing and moaning.

I nodded my sympathy at each as I approached Daddy. "I'm sorry," I said, shaking his hand. "Thank you for comin', Chaplain."

I wound up sitting next to the youngest daughter. Shortly after I sat down, the door opened. In stepped the third daughter, a look of angry puzzlement on her face.

Seeing the inevitable news on the faces of everyone in the room, she started shaking her head "no." She crossed her arms and backed into the corner, oblivious to the fact that if the door swung open she would get smashed. She looked across the room at her oldest sister. A look of rage came across her face. "DON'T YOU LOOK AT ME THAT WAY!" she bellowed.

The second sister's sobs turned into the gagging of someone about to throw up, and, looking for somewhere to do just that, she stood up. Beside me was a small, green, metal trash can. She was headed for it.

Quickly, I shortened her trip, moving the trash can in front of me. She fell to her knees and began dry heaving as I steadied the can below her face.

Daddy looked at me flatly and with an equally flat voice said, "Chaplain, will you say the 23rd Psalm?"

The 23rd Psalm. It sounded like a familiar title. But what was it?

*Four score and twenty years ago . . . .* No.

*I pledge allegiance to the . . . .* No.

I looked at the nurse who was standing wide-eyed near the door. Gesturing an opening book with my hands, I mouthed "Could you bring me a Bible?" She nodded emphatically, grateful for a reason to leave the room.

From the look on the third daughter's face, I thought we were not too far from a fist fight. I was confused. What was behind all the hostility that seemed to supersede the grief of losing one's mother? Why was the family sitting here surprised by a death that seemingly would be a relief that their loved one's suffering was over?

The next day during morning staff meeting, I recounted the fiasco. First I described the one sister's yelling fit. One of the senior staff, with the voice of a veteran, wryly intoned, "There is a way of telling, by the amount of yelling, who did the least for the deceased." I thought about that for a moment. Hmm. In the three weeks I had visited the family, I had never seen the third sister until she walked into the room after her mother died.

During case review later that week, I raised my question about the family lingering at the hospital longer than any other family with which I dealt during a death. My supervisor asked me to describe some of the other deaths at which I had been present in the short two months I had been at the hospital. All but one had been a sudden unexpected death such as a heart attack. The only one that came after a chronic illness had been the first death to which I was called, and the family's pastor had arrived shortly after I arrived, and I had left. My supervisor said, "So, all those sudden unexpected deaths; what emotion do they all have in common that death after a chronic illness doesn't have?" I thought for a moment. "Shock?" My supervisor nodded. "People who are in shock just go on autopilot. But when a death has been coming for some time, there is nothing but raw emotion." (This lesson would later explain the most painful grief reaction I saw during my residency. A teenage girl was ushered by myself, a nurse, and some other family members into the room where her long-ill mother had died. The girl threw herself on her mother. The girl's weight forced air from her mother's chest, make the sound of an exhale. The girl leapt back, glared at us as if we were cruelly lying to her, pointed at her mother and screamed, "She's alive!!!")

The nurse returned with the Bible. I vaguely recalled that Psalms was in the middle of the standard Gideon Bible, which I had never known to contain the Apocrypha. At my ordination, the pastor of the church had presented me with a new Bible just before I was to read the scripture passage for the service. I had attempted to open the Bible to 1 Corinthians, but the first book I found was Second Esdras. There didn't seem to be enough room to the right to contain the New Testament *and* the appendices I knew this study Bible to contain, so I thought this Bible had appended the Apocrypha to the end, and I turned pages far to the left. Tobit. Maybe the New Testament was at the end. I thumbed far to the right. Fourth Maccabees. I thumbed back to the left. Judith. The pastor blurted out loudly enough for everyone in the small 150-seat sanctuary to hear, "It's in the NEW Testament, Brad." Everyone had laughed.

Now here I sat unable to remember the first phrase of the 23rd Psalm. Surely I could find it and read it. Or could I?

I found it. I read it. We prayed.

We shuffled to the room.

Usually this was the point where families each kissed the deceased and left. Not this time. A little over three hours after I had left home, I got back. Connie had reheated my dinner while I was en route.

The next year I began my tenure as associate pastor for youth and young adults at a church in the same city. One of my first efforts was starting a Sunday night book study for young adults. Due to its popularity at the time, and my having been through a study of the book at a previous church, we started with Stephen Covey's *The Seven Habits of Highly Effective People*. Rachel, one of the participants in the class, was a young professional woman who became very enthusiastic about how the study helped her. She became one of my greatest advocates, inviting others to attend and offering me encouragement. She was in the middle of a three generation family in the church, with her parents being charter members and her own children now growing up in the church. I became very close to the whole family who generously gave their time and resources in chaperoning youth functions, washing cars, and hosting events in their homes. Sadly, their level of involvement was interrupted when Rachel's mother was suddenly diagnosed with a very aggressive form of cancer. She only lived a few months.

The call came while I was in a meeting in the pastor's office. Mrs. Jacobs' death was imminent. The pastor and I immediately began the ten minute drive to Veteran's Memorial Hospital. One mile to the bypass. Half a mile to the flyover to the main interstate. Just when we got past the point of no return on the flyover, we saw that the traffic on the interstate was at a dead stop. We came to a stop three quarters of the way across the flyover. Less than a mile away we could see the exit to the hospital. It might as well have been 20 miles away. After ten minutes I started walking to cars behind me until I found a woman who loaned me a cell phone. I called the church and asked them to call the hospital and tell the family we were stuck in traffic with no idea how long it would take us to get to the hospital.

Veteran's Memorial Hospital. This was the hospital where I had wanted to do my postgraduate residency in Clinical Pastoral Education (CPE). I had been in Baptist institutions all my life— Baptist churches, Baptist college, Baptist seminary— and I wanted to stretch my wings over new territory. But I was not offered a position. Actually, my first choice had been to go to graduate school and pursue my PhD. My lack of enthusiasm for a full year of CPE came out in my interviews, and at the other two places where I had interviewed I was told I was an alternate. During my interview at Veteran's Memorial, the director of the program had said, "Brad, we've heard you talk a lot about yourself. Tell me about your friends. Or do you have any friends?" A pastor on the advisory board interviewing me had shot the director a smiling glance and patronizingly said, "Be nice, James." Later in the interview, the director asked me what I was most nervous about regarding the position. I told him that since I had never had a death in my family closer than a great uncle, and since I wasn't present when that death happened, I had no experience being with people in the midst of a death. He then posed a hypothetical situation: "You've been asked to inform a family that their loved one has just died; what would you do?"

I rambled through a halting, speculative answer. When I finished, the director, who had the angular austere face of the cleric villain in any movie of the Robin Hood genre, looked at me with disdain and said, "Brad, what would it have meant for you to say, 'I don't know'?"

I shrugged. "This is a job interview. I thought you wanted to know what I do know, not what I don't know."

I told that story to a colleague where I was eventually offered a position. He smiled and said, "He wanted to see if you were teachable, or if you were a know-it-all who had your mind made up about everything."

"Well, I think there was a better way to find that out than by humiliating me in front of all those people."

My colleague smiled. "Maybe that's why Janet is so unhappy working over there."

"But the day I interviewed, she spoke so highly of her experience."

"She lied. She was on the clock. It was her job to make the program look good. No wonder she's being treated for ulcers," he concluded, implying she was stressed out from the working conditions.

I could relate to being stressed out in a CPE position. When I had interviewed at one of the nation's most prestigious CPE programs in North Carolina, they asked me to describe my CPE experience in seminary. I told them I felt like it had been the spiritual equivalent of open-heart surgery without anesthesia and I had been left to sew myself back up. The interview committee expressed hope that, if I came there, they could help me complete my journey. But because of my candor in stating that my real hope was acceptance into a Ph.D. program, I was named an alternate. I was eventually offered a position, but, when I was not accepted into the Ph.D. program, I accepted the position in Tennessee, because I wanted to go home.

It also felt good to be going somewhere where I was a first choice. So I thought. Then one day in didactic, as we were wrapping up, my supervisor began relating to me and my two fellow residents how the topic of the day related to someone who had interviewed for the residency that year. "Oh," he said, "we had a great opportunity to get someone with a lot of expertise in this area. He was a Ph.D. student at Baylor who wanted to do a year of CPE. I thought we were going to get him, but at the last minute he turned us down; so we got Brad."

A day or two later in supervision, I told my supervisor how much that hurt to hear. I had promised myself I wouldn't, but I started crying. I could tell by the look in his eyes that he regretted what he had said, that it was a moment of carelessness, but at the same time he was proud of me for confronting him. "I mean, to be told in front of my peers that *I* was a second choice . . . it made me feel like the second string."

My supervisor pursed his lips and humbly nodded. "I'm sorry," he said. I thought about it as I was going home yesterday and realized what an inappropriate thing that was to say."

My pastor and I walked through the door of Veteran's Memorial Hospital. The pain of humiliation came over me as it did every time I walked through that lobby. I had been rejected by this hospital and a second choice at the others. And here I was in the very building where I was labeled a know-it-all— simply because I responded hypothetically to a hypothetical question— being faced with the reality that I had feared. In the meantime, my grandmother had died, and I had gained some personal experience with what was needed in the midst of grief.

Over the intervening years, Rachel and her sister often have recounted the events of that day from their perspective. They laugh about it now.

"The chaplain kept coming in and asking if he could do anything. We kept saying 'Are Hershel and Brad here yet? We just want to see our pastors.' It just seemed like it was taking forever. We had gotten the message that you were stuck in traffic. But we didn't want them to take Mamma until you all had been there with us. Then you all got there, and it was like, 'OK, we can do this now.'"

Granted, the original question posed to me regarded how I would *inform* a family about a loved one's death. I still have never had to do that. At the hospital where I did my residency, by policy, only a doctor could inform a family of a loved one's death. I have been present many times, but I have never actually had to give the message.

But over the years of being with families in hospital rooms and at funeral homes, I have noticed a recurring theme. Only twice has anyone said, "Thank you for what you said." Once was at the funeral of my favorite high school history teacher. I took a copy of my senior year high school annual to the funeral. I opened it to the page my teacher had signed and read it to his widow. "Brad, for many students graduation marks a setting of the sun; for you it is just beginning to rise." I told my teacher's wife that his confidence in me often helped me through difficult times. Whenever she sees me she tells me how much that meant.

Another woman lost her husband while I was in the Philippines for the summer. I knew he would die before I returned, so before I left, I wrote a letter for my parents to give her when the time came. Years later she told me that from time to time she pulled out that letter and read it.

Out of the scores of visitations I have made with people in mourning, those are the only two times anyone has said, "Thank you for what you said." Every other time, people have said, "Thank you for being here."

However, if you *have* to say something, here are some things to avoid. If I ever get run over by a truck, for the love of all that is holy, please don't send my family a spray of flowers featuring a toy phone and a banner that says "Jesus Called." (So help me, I saw this at the funeral of one of my own distant relatives.) Unless you enjoy people smiling at you patronizingly while secretly fantasizing of slapping you, don't say "Jesus needed another angel in heaven." Unless you want me or someone like me to shoot laser beams from our eyes, upon the event of the death of our beloved grandmother, do not suggest that "you shouldn't grieve the death of someone who lives to the ripe old age of 86."

If you are in a state of chronic grief (say, after prolonged infertility) and you want to put a stop to insensitive comments and nosey questions, I have found that "thank you for your concern" does not work. However, there is something you can say that will make its way through a family and/or community faster than kudzu through an abandoned lot. Hypothetically speaking, if you are at a funeral and your spouse's biddy great aunt twice removed loudly retorts in front of several people "Your daughter is four! Four!? Well, it's time to have another one. Let's get with it! When are you going to have another one?" We may ask ourselves why people think the reproductive plans of others are any of their business in the first place. Then we may ask ourselves why otherwise prudent and prudish people will ask a question inherently raising the issue of sex and then be surprised if you answer their question. Thus, if someone asks, "When are you going to have another one," they likely will turn blood red and flee if you say something like, "Well, I suppose if we ever start having unprotected sex again," or "Whenever one of my sperm fertilizes one of her healthy eggs and it successfully implants in her uterus rather than in a fallopian tube." If, hypothetically, you are a male and you say this while sitting next to your wife at a funeral, after the biddy aunt flees up the aisle, your wife may slip her arm in yours, lean over and gently whisper, "I *love* you." And the people in adjacent pews, now staring awkwardly straight ahead will soon report the incident to complete strangers on the street and everyone in town will stop asking you when you are going to have another child or making comments like "just be happy for the one you've got."

There is an old adage that says, "If you don't know what to say, it is better to remain silent than to speak and give evidence of the fact." But, especially in the context of grief, there is something much more dangerous than speaking when we don't know what to say; it's speaking when we think we know exactly what to say. So whether we don't know what to say, we've forgotten what to say, or we think we know what to say, usually the better part of valor is to ask a question rather than make a statement. When I was walking through the valley of the shadow of my grandmother's death, rather than telling me to be thankful that she lived to be 86, I wish my church friend would have asked "What will you miss most about your grandmother." I might have said something like, "Right now I'm missing the fact that she died while I was en route to visit her with our 3-day old daughter whom we named for her. I had looked forward to laying her first namesake in her arms, and I missed that opportunity by 1 hour and 45 minutes." My friend might then have said, "I'm so sorry." I then would have said, "Thank you" and felt in the presence of a shepherd rather than a wolf.

**Questions for Reflection**
1) If people appreciate us "being there" in times of pain, what compels us to feel that we must say something?
2) What would be a less hostile way to respond to an intrusive question or statement (rather than lashing out)?

# CHAPTER 4

## The Godly's in the Detailing

I arrived at my car from a grueling day. If stress shortens life, I had let this day whittle a goodly amount from my mortal existence. My stark white, twelve-year-old, 1982 Nissan Sentra was glowing cherubically. I parked each day in the gravel lot on the east side of the hospital. So my car usually was covered in gravel dust. I was sure that was the way I had left it. I looked inside. The dash shone with polished luster. In the driver's seat on a piece of paper was a smiley face drawn in my wife's handwriting. I opened the door and breathed in a well-detailed car.

I had been interviewed that day for promotion from basic to advanced status as a Clinical Pastoral Education (CPE) resident. It was everything of the grilling it was billed to be. After my interview I had opted to stay in the room while they talked about me. It was odd to be talked about in the third person with me sitting there.

"From the moment he walked in, he gave you a lot of power," said the bearded supervisor from another city, speaking to my supervisor. "Yes," agreed another guest interviewer. "What was it? Oh, yes, that comment about letting you have your usual *throne* when we were picking our seats."

I hated the CPE modus operandi. Every little movement dissected to the n[th] degree. Every word indicted under suspicion of nefarious motives. Good-cop and bad-cop wearing clerical collars instead of badges.

I left the hospital convinced I had failed. I agonized until my supervision meeting the next day. I conceded to my supervisor my anxiety. I had learned long before that hiding anything was futile. He was like

Hannibal in *Silence of the Lambs*; he could smell fear, anger, and sadness and sometimes, I thought wrongly, he preyed on it. One day he had asked me what I was mad about. I denied being angry. He pressed me. I continued to deny it. "I'm not mad!" I said. "THERE!" he said, pointing at my foot. "What did you just do with your foot?"

"I don't know."

"You tapped it on the floor."

"So?"

"That's a gesture of anger. You said, 'I'm not mad,' but you smacked your foot on the floor."

"Well, I'm mad *now* because you keep berating me about what I'm mad about!"

"But you've been smacking your foot on the floor the whole time you've been talking. Now what are you afraid will happen if you tell me you're angry?"

I paused, then admitted: "You'll be mad at me for being mad at you."

He continued to usher me toward being congruent with my feelings. I needed to be able to trust that he was on my side, that it was his job to evoke my feelings so I could deal with them.

I had become much more congruent with my feelings in the meantime. So now, I was just going to tell him that it hurt to feel like a failure. I feared that my peers would both be moved to advanced status, but I—the one who was an alternate in the first place—would still be at basic status.

My supervisor smiled, took out a pen and two pieces of paper and began writing on them. He handed me one of the pieces of paper and told me to put a check by the option I felt reflected my status regarding the advancement interview.

I looked at the paper. There were three options: Did not pass; Passed with reservations; Strongly passed. I marked "Passed with reservations." I looked up. My supervisor extended his folded slip of paper in one hand while opening the other to receive mine.

We traded. I held my breath and unfolded the slip. "Passed with reservations." I looked up. He was smiling compassionately.

"What were your reservations?"

I told him.

"Those were mine, too," he said with a smile. We were on the same page. "Let's work on those," he said. I smiled and nodded.

At the end of my residency, and at the same time I was beginning my tenure as associate pastor at a church, I started the process to become a licensed marriage and family therapist, becoming an intern with a certified family therapy supervisor. My church knew of my need for clients to accumulate the required contact hours and would refer friends or, sometimes, would approach me with their own concerns. My experience in my family therapy internship heightened my awareness of issues of abuse and the precarious balance that ministers face in advocating for families within the midst of the sensitivities of church politics. By this I mean, a church is ideally a haven. While people expect a counselor at a public counseling center to report suspected abuse issues to authorities, the minister/member relationship involves a sacred trust for which the possibility of a false accusation has far wider implications than for a public agency. For example, someone might say, "I wouldn't go to that church; I heard the minister reported Mrs. Jones for child abuse, when Johnny had simply fallen out of a tree." If you think a government agency is obliged to protect the identity of someone reporting a suspicion, that is true. But . . . if Johnny's mother asks Johnny why anyone would think she abused him, and he says he told the minister because he was mad at her . . . word has a way of getting around.

Thus, I felt very awkward one night at a weekly church dinner. I was enjoying my spaghetti when I overheard a conversation right beside me between parents discussing discipline issues. A mother matter-of-factly boasted that she knew how to handle her 12-year-old son. "He sassed me the other day. Bad idea. Especially wearing a pair of shorts. I went outside and cut me off a switch, and I wore the back of those legs out. About that time, my dad called, and I told him what had just happened. He said, 'Good for you, honey. It's about time.' And then he came over to the house to see my handiwork. He looked at those red marks on his legs and told Bobby he hoped he learned his lesson."

I was horrified. I believed the behavior I just heard described constituted abuse at worst and un-Christian cruelty at the least. Still, I knew in Tennessee the law would not consider a switching to be abusive. Should I say something? What should I do?

I scheduled parenting conferences. I made extra efforts to invite these and other parents I thought would benefit most. However, my experience has been that those who would most benefit from marriage and parenting conferences usually are the ones who won't participate.

In this case though, the mother eventually called me for help. Her son was failing in school. Her youngest son had been suspended from school for calling one of his male teachers a queer. The mother associated the younger son's behavior with his following the example of the older son's "attitude problem." I asked if I could come to the house and we could all meet together. That would be fine.

We had the usual preliminary chit chat about pictures on the mantle and beautiful family heirlooms. But the tension was thick around the den as we took our seats. The younger son was absent. The older son glared across the room at his mother. The stereotypically laconic father struck me as the "can't we all just get along" peacemaker in the family.

Mother read the indictments. Bobby was not applying himself in school. He was failing, making Ds and Fs. He did not help around the house. "The other day when they were out of school, I came home from work and he had drunk an entire case of 12 Cokes. I said I wasn't going to buy anymore and he went off on me."

I can't remember all the details of the nearly one hour conversation. But I vividly remember that the mother's main concern was Bobby's failing grades in school, and I vividly remember the way that theme played out in the last few minutes of our discussion. I asked Bobby what he liked about his father. Bobby rattled off a litany of qualities he admired in his father and activities they enjoyed engaging in together: hunting, watching NASCAR, playing video games, etc.

Then I asked him what he appreciated about his mother. He became sullen and shrugged. There was a long awkward silence. Finally I prompted. "Come on, there must be something you appreciate about your mom."

He shrugged, scowling at her. "She cooks . . . sometimes."

I looked across the room at the mother. She had locked eyes with her son, but now appeared to be the one under indictment.

Carefully, respectfully, compassionately, I ventured: "Jane, what grade would you give yourself as a mother?"

"Well, I would have said a C, but after hearing that, it sounds like I'm getting an F."

I glanced over at the son. A scornful . . . but . . . relieved? . . . grin had replaced the blank sullenness. *Well, well, well. I'm not the only one getting an F on my report card* he seemed to be telepathing.

I didn't want Jane to be overwhelmed. I threw her a line. "I know it's got to hurt to hear Bobby not say anything. But I think this is one of those times that is like having a stomach virus. You know: when you are nauseated and you can't remember what it's like to have an appetite, and you can't imagine ever wanting to eat again?"

"Yeah."

"You all are having a tough time right now. And it's hard to remember the good times. Bobby's mad right now. He feels painted in the corner about his grades. I remember my dad screaming at me one day because I wasn't applying *myself* in school. He was making me take an advanced level class I didn't want to take. I thought he was so mean. But the day I graduated from high school I thanked him for making me take that class. One of these days Bobby will come to see you really just care and want what's best for him. Right now *he* wants *you* to see that he maybe needs that communicated in a different way. Next week maybe we can talk about some specific ways to do that."

The next week about an hour before our appointment, Jane called to cancel because they had unexpected company. She said she would call and reschedule. She never did. But at the end of the semester she did call with some news. Bobby had made the B honor roll. I sensed she now assigned herself a grade of passing with reservations. And I breathed in the satisfaction of my own more polished self.

## Questions for Reflection

1) A popular self-help book suggests "don't sweat the small stuff." A folk wisdom aphorism says, "The devil's in the details." Are these contradictions or do they constitute a paradox in which both may be true depending on the context? Explain.

2) PS: A few years after initially writing this chapter, and having used this story as a 'success' story, I learned that Bobby's little brother, who NEVER caused a problem in the family when young, was in jail for stealing to support a drug habit. While I had never believed that everything had been cured in the family, I would not have predicted the seriousness of the eventual problems with Bobby's brother. Find a brief internet article on "the identified patient" and speculate on what I missed.

# CHAPTER 5

## The Slings and Arrows of Contagious Misfortunes

Anyone who is a parent knows how hard it is. You are trying to give a stern lecture to a recalcitrant pilferer of purloined candy bars, but the face of the creature before you looks more like a psychotic chocolate Easter bunny than that of anything human. Sometimes it's tough to keep a straight face. Unfortunately, most situations in a hospital require a particular need to maintain solemn composure. Sitting with a woman whose husband has just had a massive stroke is not the best time to explode laughing.

Missionary Maurice Graham was one of the 13 hostages held by Saddam Hussein in the U.S. embassy in Kuwait in 1990. Shortly after his release, I did an exclusive interview with Graham for the *Western Recorder*, the news journal of the Kentucky Baptist Convention. I only had 15 minutes, so in the interest of time, I asked Graham to free associate his memories based on my one-word prompts.

"Horror." Among other things he told me about receiving a call from the Pentagon on the embassy's still secure phone line. The hostages were told that if they were not out by a certain date, a rescue attempt would be launched. They could expect a 50 percent casualty rate from friendly fire as the invading force fought their way in. Graham was asked to take an inventory of body bags in the compound. There were not enough for 6-7 casualties. He had to order more— possibly one for himself.

I ended with the word "humor." He said, "Oh goodness! If it had not been for the hilarious things that happened we probably would have gone crazy." He told me some wonderful anecdotes. In one incident, he and two of his fellow hostages were watching from a window as three Iraqi soldiers attempted to spray-paint over some anti-Hussein graffiti across the street from the embassy. They didn't have a screwdriver to pry the cap off, so two of the soldiers held the base of the can while the other began to hit the cap with a rock. Funny what one small puncture does to a pressurized can. The soldiers ended up looking more ready for the student section at a University of Tennessee football game than for desert warfare. Graham said, "We laughed so hard we were afraid they were going to start shooting at us."

While I would not describe my own experience in the hospital as horrific as Graham's, I was in the midst of other people's horror. And I can relate to the balm of humor—both accidental and intentional—realizing, however, that it would be dangerous if I didn't hold my laughter until later.

As shown by the plethora of home-video TV shows, we don't like to see people get hurt, but there is slapstick humor in human gaffs. The advantage of watching on TV is that you've already been assured no one was seriously harmed, so it's OK to laugh.

It is *not* OK to laugh when a woman is describing her husband's stroke—regardless of the Keystone Cops and juggling, unicycle-riding monkeys performing just behind her.

It was about midnight. The emergency room intake and waiting area was empty except for myself, the graveyard-shift clerk—working her way through para-legal school—and Mrs. Elmer. It would have been totally quiet, except for the clerk's intake questions and the keystrokes as she entered Mrs. Elmer's soft-spoken but precise replies. Mrs. Elmer apparently had trained herself to keep her voice low in spite of her loss of hearing which was apparent by the frequency with which she asked for questions to be repeated.

I was sitting almost knee to knee with her in one of the stations at the intake counter, the clerk at a computer to my left, Mrs. Elmer fumbling through her purse for insurance cards. During the long lulls while the clerk entered data or was fetching a folder, Mrs. Elmer was describing in graphic detail how her husband had collapsed, barely missing the dresser they had been given by his parents when they started housekeeping 57 years before. She hoped he would be all right.

He wouldn't be. I had seen the EEG. It was a two hemisphere total bleed out. I knew they had called the code, and the doctor was washing his hands to come and tell her the bad news.

To my right, from behind Mrs. Elmer, I saw the door to the ER open slightly. A wide-eyed female nurse motioned for me to come to the door.

"Excuse me," I said to Mrs. Elmer, who had returned to telling me about her husband.

I stepped out of the lobby into the ER foyer.

"Have you told her her husband died?"

"No," I said incredulously, feeling a little defensive the nurse would think I would break the hospital policy that only doctors informed a family member of a death. "What's wrong?"

"He's back," she said.

"Who?"

"Her husband! He had been completely flatlined for like 10 minutes. We were starting to clean him up and all of a sudden the monitor started blipping! So now we have to wait for it to stop again."

I walked back and took my seat again with Mrs. Elmer.

"Did you find out anything about my husband?" she asked.

"I found out the doctor . . . is still working with him. He'll be out to talk with you in a little while."

The clerk sat back down and began asking routine intake questions again, Mrs. Elmer giving her polite replies.

Behind me, the main door exploded open. As I began to turn, I heard a man bellow, "I NEED A DOCTOR! I GOT A FISHHOOK IN MY EYEBALL!!!"

As I completed my rotation, I saw a tall, skinny, greasy man striding toward us with his left hand over his left eye. His short, stocky, and stunned fishing buddy— likely the source of the miscast hook— was humbly taking up the rear. From her seat beside me, Mrs. Elmer obliviously continued to the clerk, "His heart doctor is . . . ."

The walking beer bottle was now right beside me on the opposite side from Mrs. Elmer. "I'VE GOT A FISHHOOK IN MY EYEBALL!!!"

Continuing to type with her left hand, and not averting her eyes from her screen, the clerk nonchalantly lifted her right hand and forefinger to say "just a minute."

"BUT-I-HAVE-A-FISHHOOK-IN-MY-EYE-BALL!!!"

"He was doing SO good lately," Mrs. Elmer continued. I was trying to keep eye contact with her, but kept glancing at our newest patient and fighting the urge to rub my left eye.

"DO YOU ALL UNDERSTAND ME?! I-HAVE-A-FISHHOOK-IN-MY-*EYE-BALL*!!!"

"Sir," the clerk said flatly, "if you'll sit down, I'll be with you in just a minute."

I continued nodding my head and attempting to look empathic as Mrs. Elmer continued her paean to her husband. And then suddenly, the protective callous of shock having been worn away, an invisible knavish fiend began tickling my funny bone with an albatross feather.

Simultaneously in my mind's eye I saw the face of the nurse peering through the door, Mo and Shep walking through the door, the animatronic clerk successfully ignoring a fishhook in an eyeball, and Mrs. Elmer wading through the swamp, unaware of the gators all around. *With the appropriate soundtrack, this would make great comedy!* I bit my lip, but that wasn't where the fiend was applying his feather. I bit my lip harder.

I suppose my struggle to keep from laughing was complicated by remembering the last time something similar had happened. That time, I had had to lower my head and pretend to be praying.

The mother of a friend of my father was on one of my units. Dad's friend was a tall man from a rural county and spoke with a thick Southern drawl, but with no bravado, a cross between John Wayne and Richard Simmons. "Braaaad Bulllll," he had said when I walked into the room the first time. "I remember you when you were thiiiis biiiig," he said, holding his hand even with the bed. He couldn't believe that I was "out of seeeminaaary."

A few days into her stay, John Wayne Simmons (J.W. for short), called me. His nephew, his mother's grandson, had died. He had lived with her, she had raised him like a son. (Apparently, though only in his twenties, he had been sick for some time, and based on the non-specific nature of the story I was hearing, it seemed the nephew's demise might have been drug related or some other nefarious complication.) Given that his mother already had a serious heart condition, J.W. was apprehensive about what the news would do to her. He told me he was coming to the hospital with his brother, and they wanted me to accompany them to the room to help comfort her when they broke the news.

I met them in the hallway outside her room at the appointed time. J.W. told his brother he had known me since I was "this tall," holding his hand out waist high. Then things turned somber as we went over the plan. J.W. would tell her. I would be there as a calming presence.

We walked into the room. I stood beside the bed on Mama's left. J.W.'s brother stood on the opposite side from me. J.W. stood at the foot of the bed.

"You remember the chaplain, Mama?" She looked at me, eyes magnified by her Coke-bottle-bottom glasses. "He's the one I knew when he was thisss big." She thought for a moment, then nodded.

J.W. began making small talk. J.W. continued making small talk. J.W. made some more small talk. J.W.'s brother and I looked at each other, wondering when the hammer would drop. There was a pause. Here it came. "Mama, there's something I need to tell you. You know Billy's been real sick. We've done everything we could to help him. But last night he had a really bad night, and he just didn't make it. Brenda found him and called 9-1-1. The ambulance came, but they couldn't revive him."

J.W. stopped his monologue. Mama was staring stoically at J.W. She looked over at me. I pursed my lips, shook my head, and mouthed, "I'm sorry." She returned her stare to J.W. as J.W.'s brother and I swapped a glance of "Hmm, not as bad as we thought."

"I'm real sorry, Mama," J.W. said, breaking the pause.

"WHAAT?"

"I'M REAL SORRY."

"ABOUT WHAT?"

"ABOUT BILLY."

"WHAT'S WRONG WITH BILLY?"

With the benefit of hindsight, this would have been a good time for J.W. to start his monologue over, just several decibels higher. But he didn't.

"HE DIED."

(I suppose the next sound struck me as funny because it sounded so much like a scene from one of my favorite movies, *A Christmas Story*. The main character has said a bad word which he claims to have heard from a certain friend. His mother calls the alleged scatologist's mother to report the infraction. The mother inaudibly whispers the offending word into the phone. Then, from across the phone line, the audience hears the other mother screech...)

"WHAAAAAAT!"

Then Mama began crying and saying "no" over and over and crying. But she was not hyperventilating or giving any other signs of life-threatening physical distress.

Now, I know it must sound horribly callous. Maybe you had to be there. But so help me, I was about to explode laughing. I buried my chin in my chest and pretended to be... no, I *was* praying. I was praying "God, please keep my nose from snorting and my shoulders from shaking."

Another time when I was in a similar predicament, I had a legal pad to hide behind. I was teaching youth Sunday school at an urban church I attended while in seminary. I was an aspiring counselor, so when Samantha, a middle-school aged girl, asked if she could talk to me about a problem, I tried to make it official by having a lap pad on which to take notes. I knew her family situation quite well. Her father was controlling but aloof, and her mother was a workaholic consumed with the latest fashions and keeping up the charade that her oldest son was driving a customized BMW because she was doing very well in her business and not because he was a drug dealer. Samantha had recently been suspended from school for cursing a teacher in front of her class. Samantha's father reacted by blaming the teacher and moving his daughter out of public school and into an exclusive private school, "where she should have been in the first place."

In the course of a rather boastful "confession" about her exploits, Samantha matter-of-factly announced that she had "attention deficit disorder." I interrupted. "A doctor has diagnosed you with A-D-D?"

Samantha looked puzzled. "No." She regained her balance and effervescently said, "But ALL my teachers have said they think I've got attention deficit. My PARENTS think I have attention deficit." Then she added the big coup for her Sunday school teacher's benefit: "Even [my youth minister] thinks I have attention deficit." She sighed, then nodded emphatically. "And I have to agree with them, because I don't think I get enough attention."

I guess I looked odd trying to take notes holding my lap pad up in front of my face. I bit my lip and focused on keeping my shoulders from shaking.

I know there are people who genuinely have a neurological disorder that impedes their ability to concentrate and persevere at tasks. But in Samantha's case, I couldn't help but think, "Out of the mouths of babes. Somebody finally hit the nail on the head."

But obviously it would have been the epitome of bad taste and very unprofessional to have allowed myself to laugh openly in the situations with Samantha, Mrs. Elmer, or J.W.'s mother. Laughter may be "the best medicine" according to *Readers' Digest*, but it is a medicine easily abused and very dangerous. Sometimes the medicine is mis-prescribed by the one laughing at someone, and sometimes simply is inappropriately taken by someone who just needs to lighten up. In my experience, unappreciated laughter rarely has more devastating effects than it does at church. Maybe this is because people see church as a sanctuary, where they are not supposed to be hurt, so any insult seems magnified.

I have seen laughter mis-prescribed both intentionally and unintentionally in church. In a church where I was a member, I once saw a pastor intentionally say something to draw a laugh. He did not intend to hurt the person to which his remark was directed, but I saw the hurt in the man's eyes. It was in a Sunday morning worship service, with a full sanctuary. The pastor was attempting to honor a large, robust Sunday school teacher for several years of service. The pastor said, "I wasn't here when he started teaching. But I'm told that John started teaching his class twenty years and 4 belt notches ago." Years later, the subject of the former pastor came up, and the man told me how much the comment had embarrassed him.

While it is easy to see the recklessness in joking about someone's weight, we can imagine that we will make an effort to be more sensitive and prudent. But what about accidents? For me, the part of parish ministry that invokes the most fear revolves around two similar tasks: mingling and making announcements. Both of these tasks involve the same fears: will I speak and make eye contact in a way that is appropriate? (If I don't speak to Mr. Curruthers, he will feel slighted.) Will I remember to say the right things? ("How's your mother? ... Oh, yes, I knew she died last year. I was thinking of Mrs. Witherspoon.") Will I make an innocent remark that is taken the wrong way?... as one of my childhood pastors once did.

Mrs. Polly had been attending our church for several months. She was a portly woman in her mid-fifties. She attended alone. One day, during the invitation at the end of the service, she came forward to join the church. She had the perfunctory talk with the pastor who held Mrs. Polly's hands in both of his. He directed her to the front pew where the beaming church clerk stood waiting with a golf cart pencil, a miniature clipboard, and a carbon copy membership form that the pastor would use to introduce Mrs. Polly and the nature of her decision: profession of faith, transfer of membership from a sister church, or rededication of her life to Christian service.

Mrs. Polly apparently had been wrestling with her decision and had come forward during the second verse of the invitational hymn. She and the pastor had been talking during the third verse, leaving only one more stanza for her to complete the paperwork. When the hymn concluded, the pastor might ask for a verse to be repeated or for the instrumentalists to play quietly while the congregation prayed about their own decisions. But this time the pastor saw an opportunity to re-visit the importance of an upcoming event. He gestured for the congregation to be seated. "Let me take a moment to make an announcement while Mrs. Polly finishes filling out her slip."

Unfortunately the pastor paused. And blushed. "I mean . . . your membership form." Someone snorted.

The Sunday she joined our church was the last time Mrs. Polly attended.

We may empathize with Mrs. Polly's humiliation. Other people just seem to need to lighten up. When I was in high school I once asked my mother why I had not seen Pamela at church in a long time. Pamela was an attractive thirty-something divorcee. She had been a member of our church about a year and had become a faithful member of the choir. My mother sighed. "Oh, goodness. I'm afraid she got her feelings hurt."

"How?"

"One night at choir practice we were singing a song where the altos were supposed to say "lah lah" or "ahh ahh" or something like that. Someone complained that because of the note we had to hit the sound was too hard to make. Mr. Bowman said we could change it to something easier. People started making suggestions, but none of them worked any better. Then Pamela... (Mom smirked, lowered her chin, still embarrassed that it *was* funny) ... then Pamela got all excited and said, "I know, let's all 'doo-doo!'"

The choir had exploded in laughter. Pamela never came back to church. Another casualty of friendly-fire, fired upon in the embassy of God.

**Questions for Reflection**
1) To what issues are people particularly susceptible to getting their feelings hurt if teased?
2) If someone in your church or organization is the subject of laughter, what could you do to follow up with that person? How far do you pursue someone who leaves under such a circumstance and how should that be done?

# CHAPTER 6

## What You Goose On Earth Shall Be Goosed in Heaven

As the long-running TV show *M.A.S.H.* demonstrated, practical jokes are rarely as funny as they are when they offer a sharp contrast to the surrounding context of human tragedy. The tragedies I saw as an intern hospital chaplain were not as frequent as those in a combat zone mobile army surgical hospital during the Korean War, but like Father Mulcahy, chaplain of the 4077th M.A.S.H. unit, I saw both head traumas... and head games. In terms of being an intern hospital chaplain, the stresses of dealing with the crises faced by patients and staff often were superseded by the stresses of the residency program itself: having reports of interventions picked apart by supervisors and colleagues (even more stressful for insecure perfectionists like I was), baring my soul in a kind of group therapy called Interpersonal Relations and being picked apart by supervisors and colleagues regardless of what you said (even more stressful for insecure perfectionists like I was), attending medical staff meetings with doctors and clinicians who used important-sounding terminology to describe Mrs. Smith's diagnosis and prognosis, while all I had to report was that I had prayed for her dog (even more stressful for the dog).

Stress reaches its zenith in the unknown. Ignorance is bliss, except when you know you're ignorant. For a resident chaplain, the unknown looms largest on the first day you carry the on-call pager. When will it go off? How many times will it go off? What will be the nature of the call? Will I be able to handle it? Will I say the wrong thing? Will the doctor complain to my boss? Will the family write a nasty letter to the president of the hospital? Will I get annihilated by my peers and supervisors in case review? And how much wood *could* a woodchuck chuck if a woodchuck could chuck wood?

Chris was an easy target the first day he carried the pager. He was a student chaplain in the new batch of winter term students. In addition to the residency program consisting of three paid interns, the hospital also provided a class for local ministers. They came in for four months of classes and supervised experience that included rotations being the on-call chaplain. Chris was a wide-eyed recent seminary graduate. He had a great sense of humor and bravado— making him an easy target: either he could take a joke or he needed to learn how.

Sure enough, his bravado had melted when the pager had been handed to him at morning staff meeting. He had joked about it, but his pupils had dilated. At lunch his full swagger had returned. The pager had not gone off all morning. Did he have good karma or what?

I needed more salad. And, unfortunately for Chris, his back was to the salad bar. And there on the column next to the salad bar was a house phone. And, yes, I dialed the number. Let's see, who should I input as the number to call? The hospital president? 9-1-1? (No, that had been done. "We didn't actually think you'd *call* 9-1-1.") A local lingerie shop? Wait, what about the house phone in the cafeteria? Perfect.

I nonchalantly sat down with my salad just as the pager began its frantic pulsing. "Oh!" Chris jumped, throwing back his elbows and looking down at the pager like he'd just found a leech in his shorts. What to do now? He pulled the leech... I mean the pager... off his belt and stared at the screen. "4091," he announced. He looked around the table, asking with his eyes if anyone knew the origin of the page; coronary care? ICU? ER? We shrugged, raised our eyebrows, and shook our heads. Chris got up and headed for the house phone on the column next to the salad bar.

"I wonder who 4091 is?" Michelle, another student chaplain asked.

"Don't anyone turn around or look over there," I said. "I know who it is?"

"Who!?"

"It just so happens that 4091 is the number of the cafeteria house phone that . . . at ... this ... very moment Chris is picking up to dial."

Snorts erupted from the noses of everyone at the table. "Oh, that's wonderful!" someone said. "Give us the play by play."

"Busy. Hmm. . . . Double checks the number on the pager. Yep. Dialing again.

. . . Busy. Hanging up." I looked back down at my salad. I looked at the clock, using my peripheral vision to assure Chris was not looking toward us. He wasn't; I returned to the play by play. "Picking the receiver back up. Dialing. Hmm. That busy signal is coming awfully quick. Puzzled. Puzzled." I snorted. "He looks so scared. *What if I'm late?*'" Everyone else snorted.

"Oh, this is great!" someone said. "But I can't laugh too much. I haven't carried the pager yet. If you all do something like this to me, I'll kill you."

The play by play continued. "Hmm. Looking at the pager again. Starting to dial.... Wait. He sees it. Everybody look now."

Chris was craning his neck and squinting his eyes at the number typed on the slip of paper behind the transparent plastic window at the base of the phone. He compared it to the pager. *Now why would someone...?* He sighed and lowered his head and shoulders in defeat, avoiding looking to his left, knowing that far across the crowded cafeteria five sets of eyes at one particular table were all affixed to him. The thing is, when you're a pale red head, blushing is so vivid. Finally, with a humble grin, he cocked his left eyebrow. Yep, we were looking. And now we exploded, drawing the attention of everyone around who saw the track of our gazes so that now everyone on our side of the cafeteria was staring at Chris as he walked the gauntlet back to his seat.

"That was good," he sportingly said, nodding his head as he sat down. "That was good. That was good." He let us revel for a bit. Then: "You all know what the Klingons on *Star Trek* say. 'Revenge is a dish best served cold.'"

"Oh, no," Janet moaned. "I had nothing to do with this."

"I don't want to hear it," Chris said.

"Oh, no," Janet said. The unknown is so terrifying.

Revenge being best served cold and the surprise of the unknown, those were the concepts that inspired Mike and me when our fellow resident, Kathy, went on vacation two weeks before the end of our residency. Mike and I would be leaving, Kathy would be staying for a second year.

I had gone on vacation first, nearly two months before. Mike had gone two weeks after me. When I had come back, I walked into the office the three of us shared, and a WANTED poster hung over my desk. An unflattering picture of me served as the identifying portrait. The text said I was WANTED after failing to show up to preach in chapel. (Ha Ha. Very funny. So I forgot to show up and preach the chapel service ONE Sunday morning. So the Sunday service was usually televised over closed circuit to all the bedridden people who couldn't come to the chapel. Cut me some slack; I had been up half the night. It's not like there weren't half a dozen church services on regular TV.)

When Mike went on vacation, Kathy and I rearranged his desktop and linked all his paper clips together. It was a tough week, we weren't on top of our game.     Unfortunately for Kathy, while she was gone on vacation, Mike and I were very much on top of *our* game. During morning staff meeting on her second day back, someone asked Kathy what we had done to her.

"Oh, they were awful! I mean, I knew they were going to be, but gosh! They took all my files out of my drawer and got them out of alphabetical order. It took me thirty minutes to fix them back."

"Well I'm glad my staff is using the hospital's time so efficiently," the director mockingly scolded, smiling at the camaraderie of his residents. Mike and I smiled at each other, knowing that we would be long gone before the *real* trap was sprung. The files in the file cabinet were just a distraction.

Now, you need to know two things. First, Kathy had bought a set of hardback Bible commentaries of which she was immensely proud. Second, she always started writing her sermons about an hour before chapel. I guess there's a third thing you need to know: the hardback commentaries were covered with shiny, paper dust jackets, the kind that are easy to remove . . . and replace. You could even replace them . . . on another volume in the set. It was a little challenging getting some of the jackets to fit volumes of different sizes. But this was necessary so that once discovered it would not be as simple as swapping the jacket on Psalms with the jacket on Jeremiah. And if you mix Old and New Testament, it makes it even more challenging . . . but also more rewarding.

We also left "calling cards" in every single volume. Then we put them back on the shelf in nice neat order from Genesis to Revelation. At least that's what the dust jackets said.

That was the second week of August. The first week of October I was sitting at my desk in my new office at my new job at a church on the opposite side of town from the hospital. "Brad, line two is for you," the church secretary called over the intercom.

I punched the button for line two. "This is Brad," I said, not realizing my left ear was about to never be the same.

"I AM GOING TO KILL YOU!!!"

I jerked the receiver away and shook off the pain which was somewhat anesthetized by the pleasure of it all. "Hey, Kathy. What's wrong?"

"DON'T GIVE ME THAT!" she yelled. "YOU KNOW EXACTLY WHAT'S WRONG!" She began to laugh. Then she graciously allowed me to gloat by giving me the details. "FORTY-FIVE MINUTES! I had FORTY-FIVE MINUTES to get my sermon ready. MORE than enough time. All I have to do is walk across the street to the office, read a few pages from the commentary on my text from Jeremiah, and then I can weave the sermon in my head as I walk to chapel. I mean I worked in broadcasting at a national news network! I can handle a tight deadline! But when I open my new commentary of Jeremiah but it IS A COMMENTARY OF *FIRST AND SECOND KINGS*, IT GETS DIFFICULT TO MEET A DEADLINE!"

She let me laugh. "You guys. I've gotta hand it to you. THAT was a work of art!"

"Thanks. Tell me more."

"At first I was like, gosh the publisher switched the dust jackets on these. Then I pulled down the one that *said* First and Second Chronicles, but it was the commentary for Psalms. I was like, "What the heck?" Then one of the index cards fell out." ("Hey, Kathy!" each card said. Hope your sermon was inspiring. Call us after chapel. Love, Mike and Brad.") "I read the card and screamed, 'NO!' I can't believe you all wrote a card for every volume," Kathy said with admiration. "Putting it in the New Testament section, now that was dirty. I ended up yanking most of them off the shelf before I found Jeremiah. There was this pile of books strewn all over the floor in the office. I mean, at the time, I was freaking out. I was SO mad. But then as I was running to chapel I thought, *gosh, I miss those guys.*"

"Well, we wanted you to have something to remember us by."

"Yeah, well, at least I didn't nearly break my neck like that maintenance guy."

I laughed as I remembered hearing a maintenance worker telling the story in the cafeteria about the maintenance crew's induction of a new employee. The brawny raconteur had his arms crossed on the table, leaning into the story, his eyes aglow.

"This kid was so green if he had joined the army he wouldn't have needed to wear camouflage. It was almost too easy. I called him over the radio and sent him down to the morgue to change a light bulb up on the ceiling. What he didn't know was that we were already down there." He paused for effect. What had they done in advance? "We got Lenny . . . You all know Lenny. . . . We got Lenny up on a gurney and covered him with a sheet. Then I called the kid on the radio and told him somebody had complained about a light bulb out in the morgue and that he needed to take a ladder down there to change it. Then the rest of us went in a closet. We wouldn't get to see anything, but we didn't need to. The kid walked in the door and saw the body under that sheet and said— something I won't say here— to a table full of chaplains. But the kid actually went up that ladder. Lenny timed it perfectly based on hearing the kid's steps going up the ladder and then stopping. Just when the kid was going to be reaching up over his head, Lenny started moaning real low like." After our laughing subsided, the raconteur continued. "That kid landed about eight feet from that ladder. I guess we were lucky he didn't break his neck. But, then, he didn't hit the ground hard, because that old boy's feet barely touched the floor."

I can relate to feet barely touching the floor. I've seen it with my own eyes.

It was at youth summer camp, a camp held on a Deep South university campus. Neil was a shy 13-year-old who was an only child being raised by an uncle and aunt after his parents had been killed in a car accident when he was three. Anyone who has ever worked with kids knows there are those who drive you crazy because they are always into mischief. Then there are kids you worry about because they *don't* get into any mischief. Neil was one of these. I wanted him to lighten up, to come out of his shell. So when he walked up to me in the dormitory hallway carrying a good-sized frog, I saw an opportunity. Now if there were just some place ... Ah! I heard the showers running in the hall bathroom. "Wow, that's a hoss of a frog. Why don't you slide it in one of the shower stalls?"

"REALLY!?" Neil sang out, his eyes bulging with glee.

I had just left the bathroom and knew that the showers were occupied by guys from another church; total strangers. "Tell you what. We'll go in there together. You slide Froggy in one of the showers and take off. I'll stay in there, and if the guy gets mad I'll tell him I did it."

"OK!" Neil said, doing a little jig of excitement.

We reconvened in the area in front of the shower stalls, urinals to our left, toilet stalls to our right. The shower stalls were walled cubicles with curtains that came to about mid-calf level. The ankles on the left were of a spindly middle schooler. He might get his feelings hurt. The ankles of the guy on the right were covered in the grey hair of an older chaperone. He might have sciatica. The guy in the middle? My money was on high school junior. Just right.

I pointed at the stall in the middle. Neil looked like ... well, a 13-year-old boy who was about to toss a reptile into the shower of an unwitting warm-blooded city dweller. He could not have looked happier.

I nodded assurance for the mission to proceed. Neil stealthily crept to the space between the curtain and the floor. All toes were facing away from us. No one would see. Neil laid Froggy on the floor at the base of the curtain and gave it a gentle nudge. Feeling the call of the wild it lept away from its captor. A split second later Neil was probably in the door facing of his room, ready to duck inside. My head was leaning out of a toilet stall. Froggy leapt three times before grazing a leg. Then the rain dance began in earnest, complete with whooping and hollering. And the bouncier the dance, the bouncier the frog, and the bouncier the frog, the more walls the dancer pirouetted into until finally spinning out through the curtain.

I emerged from the toilet stall pretending to fasten my belt. "What's wrong?"

"THERE'S A FROG IN THERE," the guy said, ripping his towel from off the curtain rod and wrapping himself.

"Yeah those things are everywhere down here," I said.

Out in the hallway, Neil, not too coyly, peeked from his door. I gave him the all clear signal. He bounced out of his room, gave me a double high five, and proceeded to jump around like he'd scored the winning touchdown in the Super Bowl. Then he ran to the courtyard and told the tale to his fellow youth group members. He achieved hero status.

At the end of the week, Neil's room key turned up missing. The university charged $25 for lost keys. Neil remembered having it while playing football in the courtyard. His peers lined up shoulder-to-shoulder and swept the courtyard until the key was found, nestled down in the grass.

It is so touching when friends stick together. And it can be so much fun punishing those who stray from fraternal responsibilities— unless the punishment backfires.

We did not want to go to the Knoxville Christian Businessmen's Association Annual Prayer Breakfast. Just because we were hospital chaplains did not mean that we wanted to get up at 5:30 in the morning to attend a 6:30 breakfast to listen to a retired FBI agent reflect on the criminals he had captured who might have chosen a better path if an entrepreneur had invested time and money in erecting moral guideposts in their lives. Now these convicts' bodies were behind locked doors. But their souls could be freed by the "power of the keys" Jesus had given the Apostle Peter: "I will give you the keys of the kingdom of heaven, and whatever you bind on earth will be bound in heaven, and what you loose on earth will be loosed in heaven."

Don't misunderstand. It was a fine message. It just did not go over as well before sunrise, especially when the orange juice was sour. As I had walked from the parking lot to the convention center, cold hands shoved in my pockets, I had intersected with a colleague and said, "I hate prayer breakfasts. Wouldn't it be more respectful to let God sleep?"

Usually the hospital president and his lieutenants attended the Knoxville Christian Businessmen's Association Annual Prayer Breakfast. But this year, the event conflicted with the First Annual Southeast Region Hospital Administrator's Roundtable, or something like that. The $250 table for the prayer breakfast had already been paid for. A sign saying "East Tennessee Baptist Hospital" would be the centerpiece of the table. We couldn't allow *Baptist* Hospital's table at the prayer breakfast to be *empty*. Local businessmen might start going to the Methodist, Presbyterian, or Catholic hospitals. So the president of the hospital, who couldn't order *doctors* to go to the prayer breakfast, passed the edict that the pastoral care department was to attend. We were standing in the office of the director of pastoral care when he broke the news to us. Over on his wall, a pencil drawing entitled "Laughing Jesus" appeared to be laughing at us. Now as I looked around the convention hall I saw any number of faces betraying their presence in compliance with office politics. The sour orange juice didn't help. The delegation at the Baptist Hospital table had another brewing issue of office politics. One chair at our table still was unoccupied. Where was Rick, the hospital's pastoral counselor? We, the obedient, muttered against him. Our muttering was escalating even *before* we were asked to stand for the singing of the National Anthem. Any plug of restraint was pulled when the soloist sang, "Oh, say can you see by the rockets' red glare?" As we sat down, one of my colleagues muttered, "Why mention the dawns early light when the sun ain't up yet?"

We strained to repress our snorting. We looked around. No one seemed to have overheard, and there was still no sign of Rick standing at the door looking for us.

Twenty-five minutes into his address, the speaker called for local businessmen to submit their souls to the divine accountant, take stock of their lives, and make a commitment to investing their lives paving the road less traveled rather than the road of good intentions. Commitment cards and pens were on the center of the table. Tom, one of my colleagues picked up one of the cards and examined it. He leaned over and pointed at the options, then whispered, "I'm concerned about Rick. I think somebody who wouldn't come to a prayer breakfast probably isn't saved." Fortunately we were sitting in the back corner of the hall; no one was behind me to be distracted by the pinching of my nose and shaking of my shoulders.

Tom filled out the card with Rick's name, listing his office at Baptist Hospital as the address. What decision did Rick want to make? Surely Rick needed to talk with someone about what it means to become a Christian.

Tom later said his plan had been to lay the card on Rick's desk. But by the end of the prayer following the message, Tom and I both forgot about the card lying on the table behind Tom's unfinished croissant.

The two retired men in permanent press suits showed up a week after the prayer breakfast. I happened to be alone in the main office. They were standing in the doorway, Bibles in hand, disapproving looks on their faces.

"May I help you?"

The taller man said, "We're looking for a Rick . . ." he looked down at a card in his hand, "Harrison?" I looked at the card and reflexively gulped. The man continued, "Is that his office next door?" referring to the door with the sign that said "*Pastoral* Counselor" and a sliding panel revealing the words "In Session."

"Yes," I said, matter-of-factly.

The two men exchanged glances that were both irritated and mournful for the eternal souls of someone who would make light of their mission.

I continued to feign ignorance. "He's in session right now. May I take a message?"

"No, that's alright," the taller one said. "Thank you."

As soon as they walked away I collapsed in the desk chair, put my head in my hands and focused on slowing my heartbeat, breathing a sigh of relief. They had headed toward the lobby rather than the hospital president's office. Hopefully these two fine Christian men would not be vindictive enough to make a telephone call either.

At the end of the day as everyone came into the main office, I asked if we could convene in the director's office. I shut the door. "Rick, you had two visitors today."

"Really? Who?"

"They were from the… " (at this point I looked at Tom) "Knoxville *Christian Businessmen's* Association."

"Oh, no!" Tom said. "They didn't."

"Yep."

"Did I leave that card on the table?"

"Apparently."

Inquisitive looks filled the room.

"Well, Rick," Tom said. "Since you didn't come to the prayer breakfast, we were concerned about your spiritual well-being and figured you might want to talk to somebody about becoming a Christian."

The room exploded in laughter. And over on the wall, Jesus laughed with us.

**Questions for Reflection**

1) What distinguishes a cruel practical joke from good clean fun?
2) To what Biblical passage is the title of this chapter an allusion? Revisit question #1 in light of your interpretation of that passage.

# CHAPTER 7

## Death, Proctologist Appointments, and Weddings

THE NURSE AND I LOOKED AT EACH OTHER NERVOUSLY. The rookie doctor was blowing it. In retrospect, I, the rookie chaplain, blew it by not doing more to help the doctor when I realized he was blowing it.

For the last hour, the elderly woman, sitting with her sister in the ER family consultation room, had been telling me about her husband. It was 8:00 in the morning. My pager had gone off while I was in the shower in the on-call chaplain's room. In her haste to follow the ambulance in her car, Mrs. Chesterfield had pulled on a floral bath robe over a t-shirt and pair of polyester pants. Gnarled toes with flaked red nail polish poked from her pink terrycloth scuff-style house slippers. Periodically I had gone to check on her husband's status. The last time I went, I found out he had been dead about 5 minutes. "How is he," she had asked when I came back. "The doctor is on his way to talk to you." Once again, I was in the awkward position of knowing information I could not share due to hospital policy that only the doctor inform family members of a death.

I surveyed the room. Two boxes of Kleenex; check. (Well, OK, in deference to the folks who make Kleenex, it was not Kleenex; it was some off brand stuff that was a texture somewhere between mom-and-pop-gas-station paper towels and damp newspaper.) Pager turned to silent mode; check. Identify target area of floor at which to lay widow in event of fainting; check. Size-up nurse for preparedness for dealing with this situation; . . . *uh oh, I don't know this nurse; I've never even seen her before.* She had come in while I was gone. We exchanged greetings with our eyes and head bobs. I didn't want to introduce myself to the nurse and make our guests think we were not a well-polished team. The nurse did not introduce herself to me, *so at least she knows that much.*

The doctor, a newbie like me, entered the room, looking remarkably fresh for a guy who had probably been up all night. He smiled politely and tenderly as he shook Mrs. Chesterfield's hand. Mrs. Chesterfield introduced Dr. Green to her sister as if they were at a Sunday tea. She smiled brightly as Dr. Green took a seat beside her. The nurse and I exchanged worried glances. Dr. Green's face had— somewhat— said "I'm sorry," but his mouth had not. Had Mrs. Chesterfield not picked up on the doctor's non-verbal "I'm sorry"? Had she thought he meant "I'm sorry you're at the hospital so early in the morning for such a minor thing as this has turned out to be"? Or was she in profound denial or simply remarkably quick at moving through the stages of grief? Or was Dr. Green's non-verbal communication simply clearer to us because we knew what was going on?

"What happened?" Dr. Green inquisitively asked Mrs. Chesterfield, apparently wanting to expand the base of scientific knowledge regarding the precursors of a massive fatal stroke.

"Well," Mrs. Chesterfield began, with all the drama of a proper Southern Belle. "I was fixing breakfast, and Mort was reading the paper. All of a sudden I heard a grunt. It wasn't real loud, just a 'uh.' I thought he was just reacting to something he read in the paper. I said, 'What is it?' but he didn't answer. I was starting to turn around when I heard a loud clump." As if she were doing a radio description of a ballet, she said, "When I turned around he was lying in the floor shaking and jerking." She knitted her eyebrows, but she was smiling. "I said, 'Oh my goodness. Mort! Honey!'" She half leaned down to pantomime kneeling by her husband. "I thought I'd better call 9-1-1. So I called them. And the woman asked me a lot of questions. She asked me if he was talking. I told her he wasn't. She asked me if he was breathing, and I told her he was and that his eyes were closed, but I could feel his heart beat."

She went on like that for nearly 10 minutes, describing in flowing narrative detail everything from the reason she had "yanked on" this particular robe to thinking the car wasn't going to start. (She had been telling Mort they needed a new battery now that it was getting colder.) The nurse and I kept exchanging glances. Well, Dr. Green *had* asked, "What happened?"

Finally Mrs. Chesterfield's narrative account of her husband's collapse and transport to the hospital arrived at "and now here we are."

Dr. Green smiled patronizingly. The nurse and I looked at each other. Was the doctor ever going to tell her? "Well," he said, "the chaplain is here for you...." The nurse looked at me and ever so subtly gritted her teeth and drew back her mouth, making a face that said, "Uh oh." The doctor stood and continued, "If there is anything any of us can do for you, please let us know." The women and her sister stood and shook Dr. Green's hand, each smiling and taking his hand in both of theirs, (thanking him for saving Mort?). The nurse and I nervously looked at each other again. I remembered the last time I had intervened in a doctor's action. My boss had said, "Good work. Don't ever do it again." The doctor was headed to the door. I supposed I would follow him out and tell him I didn't think Mrs. Chesterfield realized her husband was dead. She was going to have to be told. And given that she apparently interpreted the doctor's demeanor as saying everything is OK, her bubble of hope was about to be burst in an unbelievable way. It was going to be ugly regardless. The question now was how I could help pad the fall as much as possible. What could I do?

"Dr. Green?" Mrs. Chesterfield asked. *Uh oh. Too late.*

"Yes," he saccharinely replied, turning from the door.

"How *is* my husband?"

Dr. Green looked like he had just received an unexpected probe of his prostate— with us watching. Based on his baby faced appearance when he entered the room I would not have thought it possible that his face could grow more pale. I was wrong. The blanch of his face was even more stark in contrast to the red glow now radiating from the tops of his ears.

"Umm…. I'm… sorry. He… died." He didn't say it with words but his voice said, *Did I not tell you that?*

*Note to self: when informing a person about the death of a loved one, make sure to mention the loved one's death.*

Mrs. Chesterfield's face twisted in shock and confusion. Her sister's jaw went slack in terror. "What!?" Mrs. Chesterfield exclaimed.

"I'm… sorry," Dr. Green offered for the second time.

Then Mrs. Chesterfield erupted. "OH NO! NO. NO. NO. NOOOOOOOOO!"

She collapsed into her chair, convulsing. Her sister, also sobbing, knelt beside her and embraced her.

The nurse and I looked awkwardly at the pattern in the carpet. Beside us, Dr. Green stood— metaphorically speaking— with his scrubs and under shorts around his ankles, feeling more exposed and vulnerable than if he'd just gotten a proctological exam in front of a room full of medical students.

In a moment like that, you can't help but be torn between pity for the grieving person and the fearful thought *I'll never hear the end of it if this gets out.*

When it happened to me, I nearly fainted.

Mind you it wasn't a death. It was worse: a wedding.

When, as a teenager, I had made a public commitment to vocational ministry, a former pastor called to offer me his blessing and sage advice. He said, "Brad, I want to tell you two things. First, ministry is a rough road, but it is a glorious road." He then told me some examples of trials and tribulation he had faced but how he persevered and found the experiences rewarding in the long run. He started to say goodbye.

"What was the second thing?"

"What?"

"You said there were *two* things you wanted to tell me."

"Oh. Oh yeah. The second thing is this: given the choice between officiating a wedding or a funeral, take the funeral. Dead people don't complain, and there usually isn't a mother of the bride at a funeral."

Over the years I have seen the reality underlying that advice. I have seen fights break out at weddings. I once saw a bride's 10-year-old brother spit in her face. The mother of the bride dragged the boy out of the church by his ear, threw him into the back seat of a car and peeled out up the street. Then we took the pictures. Runny mascara and all. I now take a very firm hand at weddings, but that's a story for another chapter. Suffice it to say that I've seen some weddings that nearly served as the precursor to a host of funerals. One wedding nearly led to my funeral. At least I felt like dying.

It was a second marriage for the bride and groom, each in their mid 60s. Arthur, the groom, had been widowed four years before. Two years after the passing of his beloved wife, he had begun dating Stella, a divorcee of nearly 20 years. There was more than the usual amount of scuttlebutt that occurs when a widowed man begins dating one woman rather than any of the other available widows. Complicating matters was the fact that Stella had been formerly married to Billy, a best friend of Arthur and his late wife.

Arthur and Stella asked me to perform their wedding. As I did with everyone, I told them I only performed weddings if the couple had at least three sessions of premarital counseling. They agreed and scheduled sessions. It was more than a little odd counseling someone who had been married for more years than I had been alive. But there were unique elements of their merger that I was able to highlight and help them work through— like how to prepare for the reaction of their adult children.

A few weeks before the wedding, I started looking for my computer disk with my three wedding templates. I couldn't find it. Finally I gave up and pulled out the printed version from the last time I used the wedding that Arthur and Stella wanted to use.

The day of the wedding rehearsal I went through the script and crossed out every occurrence of the previous bride and groom's names and replaced them respectively with "Arthur" and "Stella." As it turned out, the last time I had used that wedding script was at my wife's cousin's wedding at Andrew's Bald, an open field at the crest of a mountain near Clingman's Dome in the Great Smoky Mountains. During *that* wedding a rain drop had hit at the top of one of the pages. I saw the effect that one drop had on the ink from an inkjet printer. Fearing the sprinkle would evolve into a freshet, for the remainder of the wedding I sounded less like a minister than an auctioneer.

*Note to self: when performing a wedding outside, test the water resistance of the script and/or laminate the pages.*

At this point you might be expecting that I got to a certain point in Arthur and Stella's wedding and the script was illegible due to the page length track of a rain drop. Nope. It wasn't even a simple incorrect letter like the very first wedding I performed for my wife's college roommate. Her husband had handed me a script and said, "I want you to read this *exactly* as it is. No ad-libbing." I took him at his word. So, when I came to the quotation of scripture that said "love is patient, love is...." *Hmm. That doesn't sound right. But that's what is written.* So I doubled back and read it as it was printed. "Love is patient; love is king...." *Love is king? That sounds like an interesting sentiment, but I don't think that's an accurate quotation.* At the end of the wedding— taking place on a 102 degree summer day in an un-air-conditioned stone chapel—I was standing on the stage in a heavy black robe watching the wedding party exit. Suddenly it hit me. *Love is KIND! Oh no. I'll never hear the end of this.* A bead of sweat formed on my neck just below my hair line. The next-to-last groomsman was escorting the next-to-last bridesmaid off the stage. When the last set of attendants was joining arms, the bead of sweat made it past the collar of my shirt. I tried to arch my shoulder blades and subtly scratch the intense itch and shake the droplet loose from the precipice of vertebrae onto which it clung. When the bride's mother was being escorted out, the droplet's death grip on my fourth vertebrae finally was broken, and it cascaded bumpitty bumpitty bumpitty down every knot on my bony back. But to my tortured amazement and agony, that droplet of sweat failed to be caught and absorbed by the elastic waistband that should have prevented the drop's arrival at its final port of call. I discreetly tightened my seat. It only made it worse. I felt every eye in the sanctuary upon me. In my mind, it wasn't because I was the only one on stage but because my face was giving away to everyone that I had an overwhelming urge to scratch in a place and in a way that prudence restrained me from doing before God and in the presence of these witnesses. (Actually it was the witnesses I was more concerned about. I figured God had seen worse. "Thou shalt not dig thy hand between thy buttocks while officiating a wedding" is not a divine injunction but a *social* convention.) However, as soon as I dismissed the congregation to the reception and they turned to exit, I dashed to the front pew, sat myself down and wallowed and squirmed like a horse rolling in dust. Ahhhh.

*Note to self: only buy underwear with high quality elastic. When it becomes stretched, buy new underwear.*

No, it wasn't a faded or misprinted word that got me. It was one simple overlooked word.

I had led Stella in her vows and was about to lead her groom in his. I had learned to write each set of vows out separately so I could turn pages straight through rather than doubling back and risking forgetting whether I was leading the bride or the groom. I turned to the first page of the groom's vows. I almost started to read, addressing the groom by the name that was the first word on the page. But at the last millisecond I stopped myself. The name of the groom didn't look right. In fact I knew it wasn't the name of the groom standing before me. It was the name of the last groom I had married using this script, the outdoorsy husband of my wife's second cousin. I knew the name wasn't right. Now if I could only remember the name of the groom standing before me right now. I scanned down the short page to see if there was another occurrence of the name that I had scratched out and written in this groom's name. Of course, I am not lucky enough for that to have been the case. I took a breath to compose myself. *Come on, Brad, you can think of it. Maybe if you look at the groom you'll recognize him.* I looked. *Oh yeah, Arthur.* "Arthur, will you commit the rest of your life to loving Stella as Christ loves the Church? ... " I made it through. At least I thought I had.

At the end of their vows and exchange of rings, Arthur and Stella descended the dais to a floor-level candelabra to merge their flames. They lit the center candle and, based on their prior decision, opted to extinguish their old selves. Then they joined hands and gazed dreamily into each other's eyes while the sanctuary was filled with a romantic ballad emanating from a pirated cassette of a top 40 song from the country charts. As I stood there alone on the stage—there were no attendants—I began reflecting on my near gaff. Something seemed particularly odd—more strange than the fact that I had nearly called him the wrong name. I had nearly called him by the name of my wife's second cousin's husband, my wife's second cousin's husband, *Billy. Oh, Lord. I nearly called Arthur, "Billy." Billy. That was Stella's ex-husband's name.* My knees went weak. A cold sweat popped out on my forehead. *Come on, Brad, please don't faint. That will just make it worse. Sure, every person in this room over the age of 12 knows that Stella's ex-husband was named Billy. I would NEVER have heard the end of that.* The room swam. The colors of the congregation's clothing swirled into an hallucinogenic blur. *NO! DO NOT FAINT! KEEP IT TOGETHER!*

At long last, our Christian cowboy minstrel finished reminiscing on grandma and grandpa's marriage, and everyone in the congregation had to stop going over shopping lists and the other mental exercises people do while two people stare at each other for three-and-a-half minutes. After prayer, a kiss, a proclamation, and a short recessional, I dismissed the congregation, and once again walked to the front pew and collapsed, though this time I sat motionless in abject terror.

*Note to self: Whatever it takes, always do a computer search of wedding scripts to find and replace all names.*

Gaffs are going to happen. My former pastor warned me about weddings because the more people who are involved in being in charge, the more likely it is that people assume someone else took care of something. Between a bride, a mother of the bride, a wedding director, a florist, an organist, and a minister, sometimes there can be too many chiefs and too few Indians. I used to hate wedding directors, especially the inexperienced flighty ones who are always out of breath and act as if the survival of human civilization hinges on the inches between groomsmen's shoulders. But at least when there's a director there is someone else to blame if something goes wrong.

I needed a director to blame the time I was hired by one of my creditors to perform a wedding for one of his employees. I was a poor graduate student and had had several hundred dollars' worth of work done to my car on an installment plan arranged with a church member who owned an auto repair shop. I was having trouble making the payments. My church member who owned the repair shop had a receptionist who was looking for a minister to perform her wedding because her minister wouldn't marry divorced persons, and this was a second marriage for both the bride and the groom. I stated my premarital counseling requirement and that I would reserve the right not to perform the wedding if I felt like the marriage was not being entered into wisely. I came to the conclusion that the marriage was being entered as wisely as anybody else's. Unfortunately, the *wedding* was not entered as wisely as the marriage.

At the usual time for such, I turned to take the ring from the ring bearer. Funny thing about the title ring bearer, you expect them to... well, bear the rings. In this case the little pillow was bare of rings. My mind raced. With the benefit of hindsight, I should have remembered the wise counsel of the minister who performed my wedding. He had said, "Now if one of you drops a ring, let's not crawl around on the floor looking for it. It may have bounced down an air duct. The congregation won't be able to see from out there. I'll just pretend to pick it up and we'll go through the motions, find the ring later, and no one will be the wiser." I should have pantomimed it. No one would have known. But NO. I suddenly remembered that the frantic bride who had arrived an hour late had shoved two small white boxes at me and asked me to put them somewhere safe. I had sat them on a shelf at the back of the "sanctuary," a large party room in a state park lodge. I told the bride and her sister where I put them.

The wedding had started a full 45 minutes late. The bride had begun putting on her dress and make up at the time the wedding was supposed to start. When we arrived at the exchange of rings, I asked the groom for the rings. He looked at me like a college freshman whose economics professor had just asked him to explain the relationship between the international monetary fund and the municipal bond market. For fear that Little Mikey, the ring bearer, would not walk down the aisle, we had decided that the groom would carry the rings and, if Mikey were there, pretend to take them from the pillow. That way, if Mikey didn't come down the aisle, we still had the rings. Seeing the confused look on the groom's face, I thought maybe the plan had changed. I looked at the ring bearer's pillow. Uh oh. I looked toward the back of the room and saw two small cardboard white boxes on the shelf over the heads of people sandwiched on the bench against the back wall. I had the sensation that my pants were around my ankles.

*Note to self regarding pre-wedding-party-entrance-checklist: "check to make sure you and groom have pants zipped" formerly was sole item. To this add: "make sure someone has the rings."*

I should have pantomimed it. But I panicked. I held up my finger and said, "Excuse me." Then I briskly walked to the back of the room (challenging with your pants around your ankles), and retrieved the boxes. Arriving back at the front, I handed a box each to the bride's mother and father. The cardboard boxes opened easily enough. But the velvet boxes were wedged in so tightly that quite a wrestling match ensued. Eventually the cardboard boxes were torn away. The velvet boxes snapped open loudly. Finally I procured the sacred bands.

For the remainder of the wedding, I felt the burning lasers of the scornful gaze of my church member who felt responsible for hiring this scatterbrained minister. At the end of the service he made a beeline for me and angrily asked, "So was the ring fiasco a result of *your* irresponsibility?" *My irresponsibility.* Not, "so what happened with the rings?" Not "were the rings your responsibility?" No. He went straight to the assumption of my *ir*responsibility. Did he say anything about my helping move and arrange chairs when rain forced the ceremony inside? No, because he wasn't there for the hour leading up to the wedding. Did he say anything about my helping scramble to attach helium balloons to all the center pieces in the reception area right up to the last minute. No, because he wasn't there. No matter how far you go above and beyond in proofreading the newspaper before it goes to press, there's inevitably a critic who will call the editor over the one typo you didn't catch. Unfortunately, some people expect fairy tales to be more perfect than newspapers. Of course there were those gracious people who said, "It wouldn't be a wedding without something funny to remember." May their number increase. But no matter how many Prince Charmings there are at a wedding, it takes just one Rumplestiltskin, who thinks every wedding should be a fairy tale, to be a party pooper. And Rumplestiltskin is usually the one who has a way with spinning straw into gold.

    I hate going to the proctologist. And I despise the goopy, water soluble residue of his encroachment. But given the choice... .

**Questions for Reflection**

1) What did my mentoring pastor mean when he said "If you ever have a choice between a wedding and a funeral, take the funeral"? In other words, what is the difference between family members' expectations and reactions at these events?

2) When I saw the doctor messing up, how might I have safely intervened without embarrassing the doctor? What might have gone badly if I had interrupted?

# CHAPTER 8

## Lock-ins are of Satan... Except When They're Not

WHEN A BOY WANDERED AWAY DURING A CHURCH HIKING trip in the Smoky Mountains, I was first and foremost concerned for his safety. But in the inner recesses of my mind, I also feared my picture prominently printed on the cover of the local paper— the young youth minister sitting on the curb with his head in his hands as, in the background of the picture, a pack of blood hounds head into the forest towing a crew of highly trained search-and-rescue personnel.

Several years before, at the first church where I served as youth minister— while I was still in seminary— I left a 6th grade boy behind when we left to go back home from a whitewater rafting trip. We had left the rafting station over an hour before, had driven down the mountain, crossed the river, had a picnic at a park, and were driving away from the park before someone on the van asked "Where's Tony?"

"In the station wagon," I said.

"No he's not."

"Yes he is."

He wasn't. I wheeled around and headed back toward the picnic area. Through the roar of gravel under our tires, I heard teenagers asking each other if they had seen Tony at the picnic. "No." "Nope." "Uh uh."

After ordering an evacuation of the van by everyone but Tony's older brother, I drove up a winding mountain road the way you drove in search of a missing child in an age before cell phones were ubiquitous commodities. As we arrived at the rafting station, a Jeep pulled up beside us. Tony was in the passenger seat. The owner of the rafting company had taken Tony down the mountain, stopping at every picnic area along the way. Tony had not been aware that we planned to cross the river before eating. I thanked the owner, apologizing profusely. Tony and his brother were typically competitive and antagonistic same-gender, close-in-age siblings. But in this moment, Tony's brother reached up to the shotgun seat, gripped his brother on the shoulder and said, "You OK, man?" Tony said, "Yeah." Then he started crying. I was baking in shame. I had been genuinely concerned for Tony's safety. Now I was also concerned about winding up in the obituaries after I faced his parents.

Actually, winding up in the paper accused of some infamous act has been one of my greatest fears while working in youth ministry. I was concerned about the youth, but I was also concerned for myself. Such was particularly the case when the church secretary solemnly told me I needed to call a certain Helen Train. Handing me the note with Ms. Train's number, Shirley said, "Her daughter was a visitor at the lock-in last weekend. She's very upset about something."

I climbed the scaffold stairs to my office and dialed the number, the phone cord coiling into a noose. "Ms. Train?"

"Yeah."

"This is Brad Bull, the youth minister at [Cooked Goose] Baptist Church. I got a message that you wanted me to call."

"That's right you did. What wuz your name uhgin"

"Brad Bull."

"All right. And I want the name of evur single chaperone you had at that there lock-in, too."

"What has happened, Ms. Train?"

"One of your little boys at your lock-in got aholt of my daughter; that's what happened."

Even now my heart is racing and I'm short of breath as I recall that moment. I had a good idea what she meant by "got aholt of." Immediately my mind did the calculus. Her daughter was pregnant. But to protect whoever got her pregnant she would say that *I* had seduced her. She would get an abortion; there would be no paternity test; it would be my word against hers. The headline in the paper would read "Local Youth Minister Accused of Statutory Rape." It would not matter how false the charge; my career would be over.

"What do you mean 'got a hold of'" I asked.

"I *mean* my daughter lost her virginity at your lock in."

I replayed the entire evening in super fast forward. We had played underground church— a game similar to hide and seek. It's a fast moving game and I had chaperones stationed patrolling with flashlights all over the building. It was unlikely, but not out of the realm of possibility. If it had happened, it was one of the fastest ever "got-aholt-ofs."

To my relief, Ms. Train named the boy whom her daughter alleged had deflowered her. The girl had confided in her older sister that she had lost her virginity. Older sister had told Mrs. Train; Mrs. Train had confronted her younger daughter who had pointed the finger at the currently accused. While she might still change her story and blame me, the accused boy certainly fit the profile for a world record conception (of the reproductive kind). Mrs. Train demanded a meeting with the parents of the boy. I told her I would meet with them and see what I could find out and would get back to her.

After briefing the pastor, I contacted the parents and set up a meeting, telling them the nature of the accusation. When I arrived at their house, Jr. looked very contrite. Dad looked smugly proud of his stud. Mom directed Jr. to tell me what happened. "Jimmy and Amy and Jennifer and I were hiding in a closet during the game of underground church. We kissed, but that was it." I'd seen him lying. He could be insolent and defiant, but his skills at lying were not yet matured. He was telling the truth.

The next day I called Mrs. Train, bracing myself to a change in story. Sure enough the story had changed, but, fortunately in a direction more favorable to my mug shot not winding up on the cover of the paper.

Mrs. Train was almost contrite. "I don't think things happened like I described them the other day. I talked with Amy and she said she was just trying to show off for her sister. She said they were just kissing in a closet, but she wanted her sister to think she had done more. So, while I know she lost her virginity, I don't think it was at your lock-in."

"What do you mean you know she lost her virginity?"

"I took her to the doctor for a pap smear. When we were driving home, I asked her if it hurt and she said, "no." (I was flummoxed by this, having never had a pap smear. I've since asked around and have it on good authority that Mrs. Train's method is not considered authoritative by any women or OBGyns I know.)

"What do you think I ought to do?"

I was so relieved I was off the hook, my defenses fell, and I said the first thing that came to my mind. "I think it would be appropriate to scare the hell out of these kids."

"What do you mean?"

"When you were at the doctor, did you request that the doctor do an HIV test?"

After a noticeably awkward pause and with a baffled voice, Mrs. Train said, "No."

"Why not?"

"Well... it was her first time."

I held the receiver out from my face and shook my head at it in bewildered awe. Returning to the conversation, I gently tried to tell Mrs. Train that (like her pap smear theory) her notion of HIV being merciful to first timers needed reconsideration and that an HIV test might be a sobering experience. She said, "OK," but I could tell it would never be done. I also knew that I'd never see Amy at church again. At the time, I selfishly thought that was a good thing. Now I wonder what I might have done differently to have dealt more redemptively with both Mrs. Train and Amy.

After that episode, however, I did make a "members only" rule for lock-ins. We would find other activities as a means of outreach. I wasn't naïve enough to believe that members wouldn't do something nefarious; after all, Jr. was a member. But I wanted to avoid any more encounters with strangers on the phone, and lock-ins seemed too volatile in the best of circumstances without throwing in folks I knew nothing about— especially if "underground church" were an activity on the agenda for the evening. Since my youth group could no longer imagine a lock-in without underground church, it would be an easy rule to enforce. Still, I rued the day I introduced my youth group to the game. It was all they wanted to do: little bands of first-century Christians, hiding from Roman soldiers empowered to imprison Christians in the Adult III Sunday school classroom (a place where few Christians survived); with one soldier being a secret and sympathetic Christian who would release captives who could return to hiding in such covert places as the preschool art supply closet.

Now one would think, given that my own earliest exploratory sexual forays happened in a church or at church activities, I would have been more suspicious about why hide-and-seek by any other name smelled as sweet to adolescents. Maybe my lack of suspicion lay in the fact that "third" base" had not yet been moved to "first base." Then again, as I write this, it occurs to me that maybe I did not want to remember the details and upshot of my own episodes of faith-based canoodling.

First base. I delivered the pitch to Ashley* and Jennifer during Sunday night fellowship meal after the evening service. All the adults were deeply engrossed in their conversations—conversations involving much laughter, soothing the worries of contemporaneous events such as Americans being taken hostage at the U.S. embassy in Iran. It was early autumn 1979. Our family had just moved to a new house and a new church. My parents had bought the parsonage that sat behind the church we were now attending. They had moved me from a large church where I was a virtual outcast to a small, rural church where I was instantly embraced by my peers. (In a diary from the time, I said that I did not want to move to a "Podunk church." But at the first youth event I attended—Jennifer's older sister's birthday party—we played a trivia game at which I excelled. At one point, a member of the other team said, "Why didn't we get the smart guy on our team?" My confidence soared. I was in a place where my strengths were admired rather than ridiculed.) I would turn 14 in December, and I was about to discover the advantage of being the only boy my age to attend evening church. All the other males were in late high school and had girlfriends. Ashley and Jennifer, the only two girls our age at church that night, went to the same middle school as I. I needed some bait to get them to want to go outside. I thought of some and posed my question. I got the answer I wanted. No, they had not seen the bulldozer sitting behind the church.

We nonchalantly slipped out of fellowship hall and headed out the side exit to the darkened parking lot. Once we turned the corner of the building to the back yard of the church, even the street lights were blocked by the building, making the rear of the building look even more foreboding.

---

* All names have been changed to protect the author.

Simultaneously Ashley and Jennifer, standing on either side of me, slid their arms around my elbows, interlinking our arms in a chain. They leaned in close to me. It was a short walk, but my life would never be the same.

For weeks I tried to replicate the experience. But Ashley did not come to evening church often, and Jennifer, for some unexplained reason, rebuffed my invitations to go for a walk to visit the bulldozer, only making me more earnestly pursue her. The nature of my pursuit changed, though, when I witnessed a slightly older couple... running... rather than walking.

Our church did not have a van, so youth outings involved a caravan of cars. On one such outing, Jennifer and I were riding in the back seat of Kevin Litton's Camaro. Dropping me off back at home, Kevin parked in the gravel lot between the church and my house. The engine had not stopped humming before Kevin and his girlfriend, Amanda, began sampling the flavor of each other's toothpaste. It looked like fun. Jennifer and I were wedged into the Camaro's small back seat. I looked at Jennifer with eyes that said, "What does your toothpaste taste like?" But she was looking at Kevin and Amanda in disgust, disappointingly apathetic about the minty flavor of my regular Crest. I, however, had now seen someone other than my parents kissing, and suddenly interlinking arms seemed less interesting to me.

A few days later Jennifer and I were standing outside the church on a brisk autumn night. We both had our hands shoved into our jacket pockets. She asked me what I wanted for my birthday. Following a premeditated plan, I nonchalantly raised the topic of my upcoming birthday party. Teasingly, I asked if she would be coming. She affirmed and then knowingly took the bait. I then delivered the most non-aggressive but unabashedly overt proposition I knew how to make. "Welllllll," I intoned, "it isn't a *noun*."

Coquettishly Jennifer asked, "Is it annnnn... adjective?"

"Nooooo."

"Is it annn... adverb?"

"Noooo."

"Well, I'm not very good at grammar. What else could it be?" She was going to make me say it.

"I want... a kiss."

Yes, in that context "kiss" was a noun. But the ploy worked, though not on my birthday. The Sunday evening after my birthday, however, just before youth Bible study, Jennifer asked me if I wanted my birthday present. After my stunned affirmation, she grinningly told me she would give it to me after Bible study.

After class we sluggishly exited the classroom, as soon as the last of our handful of classmates rounded the corner disappeared down the stairwell, Jennifer and I faced each other. She looked down at me confidently with a smile. I, the very late bloomer who did not lose my last baby tooth until the week before I turned 18, raised up ever so slightly on my toes and got verbed.

Almost a month later, the youth group had a New Year's Eve Party at my house. With revelers gathered in three different rooms upstairs, and in the basement, Jennifer and I found several opportunities to be alone in the hallway, where our verbing was joined by several conjunctions. After a few interruptions, we slipped out separate doors and rendezvoused at her sister's car. At that point we wrote an entire paragraph of passionate verbs, our skin speckled with the shadows of raindrops on the windshield.

Later, after the last guest left, my mother called me into my parents' bedroom. My father was reclined against the head of the bed. My mother was standing just inside the door, her face twisted in anger. "Your behavior tonight was completely inappropriate," she fumed.

"What are you talking about?" I demurred. It was dark outside, she could not have seen.

"I saw you out in the car with Jennifer!"

"We weren't doing anything!"

Like a bolt of lightning, her palm streaked across my face, knocking me nearly to the floor.

"Hey!" my father said scoldingly toward my mother.

Hearing his defense of me, I looked at him with pleading eyes, holding my face. He looked at me firmly, but compassionately said, "Son, you are too young to be alone in a car with a girl."

I nodded. Then looking at Mother, her eyes disdainfully and reluctantly said I was dismissed.[1]

I never kissed another girl until spring of my senior year in high school. For that matter, I only went out on four dates.

Thus, it occurs to me now that maybe I was somewhat too trusting of my youth at church, because a shadowy part of me resented the suppression of my own early romantic endeavors. Since I got my first kiss in eighth grade during the transition from youth Bible study to evening worship, and no one got pregnant, I wrongly assumed everything else would be as innocent.

It didn't take long to find out that a "members only" rule was no panacea. Though my second run-in with Jr. was not at a lock-IN but at a camp-OUT.

---

[1] I would be well into my adult years before I understood the gasoline that was fueling my mother's fire. It was gasoline that had been thrown on her. With her permission I share that when she was a youth, she suffered abuse at the hands of a family member. She handled it far better than most would. She delayed her retirement three years to pay for my house while I pursued my doctorate. Her children arise and call her blessed.

I had plenty of chaperones. (I thought. It turned out, one per tent would have been better.) The girls pitched their tents on the west end of the group campsite at the national park campground. The boys' tents were on the east end. My tent was in the middle, flaps wide open.

When we were packing up to leave, I was talking to Audrea, a perky 7th grader. I asked her how she had enjoyed her first camping trip. "I liked it a lot except for being scared being alone last night."

"What do you mean?"

A look of terror came over her face, the look of someone who just accidentally spilled the beans on some other middle school mean girls. "Oh, no! Please don't tell Marcia and Jeenie that I told you! They said they wanted to go to Sam and Ty and Ricky's tent. But I wouldn't go with them."

I decided that on Wednesday during youth group, I would do a variation on a story I had often heard my father tell. A carload of high school boys had shown up late for school, claiming to have had a flat tire. The shrewd principal had put them in four separate rooms, given them paper and pencil and said, "Write down WHICH tire was flat."

The three boys and two girls were all in attendance. I started the meeting telling the whole group we were going to play a game and that I needed five people to help me set something up. Rather than taking volunteers, I selected five. We stepped out in the hall. They looked excited. I handed each a piece of paper and a pen. "We're going to play a game called The Honesty Game." I then assigned each of them a nearby empty room to go to upon my command. Then I quickly said, "Go into your room and write an essay in which you describe EVERYTHING that happened on the camping trip between when I sent you to your tents and when we had breakfast. Then we'll see who's the most honest. Go." In between the words "honest" and "go" I saw four throats gulp. The person who did not gulp also didn't blink, just maintained his perpetual snide smirk.

When I read the essays, the person who did not gulp had written one sentence: "We went to bed and went to sleep." In the other four essays, his name was the most frequently mentioned. He was identified as the originator of the invitation and the suggestion to play Truth or Dare. The word "kiss" or some variant thereof appeared in 3 of the 4 other essays, too.

I told them that I was not going to tell their parents; they were. "You are to tell your parents what happened and have them call be BEFORE 5:00 on Sunday. Any questions?" There were none.

Sunday came. I had gotten no phone calls. After evening services we were scheduled to go to a member's home for a swimming party. I had an adult lined up to wait behind as most of the rest of us left. As the van was being loaded I called the five into the office. "Sorry gang, but you need to call your folks to come pick you up."

"What!" Mr. Oppositional-Defiant screamed.

"I told you to have your parents call me and you didn't."

"THIS IS BULLS@#T! YOU CAN'T DO THIS!"

(I was only mildly taken aback. I thought, *This is such a positive-minded church, that's probably the first time the word "can't" has been said in this office.*)

In contrast to my mental flippancy, Ty was solemn and matter-of-fact: "Knock it off, Ricky. We deserve this."

The rest of us went swimming.

*****

Then there was the ski trip.

One set of boys was not going to be allowed to go unless there was one more adult chaperone, even though I had met a reasonable ratio. One more chaperone; that was Dad's condition. I hit the phone. It wasn't going to be easy. It was a weekday when school was out for in-service training, and most of the parents had to work. I finally found a senior adult who had no interest in skiing but was willing to sit and watch.

After the van was loaded, and I made one more trip into the church, I was hastily approached by Mother. She told me to make sure her sons did not go down any black diamond slopes—that their father had made that stipulation. "I'm afraid I can't do that," I said. "It's a huge place; I can't keep up with where everyone is. If you don't want them on a black diamond slope, you need to tell them." I stared. Nodded at the van. She went.

Later in the day I was standing at the base of the slope where several trails converged. One of the Brothers skied up to me. "You want to go up with me?" I asked. "No, thanks. Joe and I are about to go up to the top of Death Wish."

I couldn't believe it. I stood there watching to see if they were actually going to get on the ski lift that led *only* to the top of Death Wish. I wanted to see... I was *hoping* they would have a last second change of heart. But they didn't. When they were the next pair to be loaded, I called their names and told them to get out of line.

They ambled over to me like penguins wearing scuba flippers. "Guys? I can't believe what I just saw. I busted my tail to get an extra chaperone so that you could go on this trip, and you just disobeyed the one instruction your mom specifically told you. Even though it would not have been fair, do you know how much trouble I would have been in if you all had gone up there and gotten hurt? Do you know how hard it would have been for me to ever get you to get to go on a trip again?"

"Are you going to tell our parents?" Ah, I had them; they betrayed their fear. I would use it. Then I pulled out a line I had learned from my high school English teacher after the Great 1984 British Literature Class Ooga-Horn-Blown-Over-the-Intercom Incident. (Ha. The guy who actually blew it is now on the school board.) "I'm too angry right now to tell you what I'm going to do." (Mrs. Finchum, realizing it was not a solitary act— due to the silence when she entered the room— had waited a week and sentenced us to bring British Christmas food to her house for a party.) I'll think about this and tell you at supper.

When we got out of the van at McDonald's, I told them to get their food and come join me. When they sat down, their faces were so filled with apprehension I had to force myself not to laugh but keep on my firm face.

"Guys, when I was in school if we got in trouble we had to write sentences. So I've decided that I'll give you a choice. I won't tell your parents, IF you'll write a sentence— a number of times to be determined. The sentence is this:..," and I handed them a piece of paper on which I had written a ridiculously long sentence that went something like this:

*When I am on youth outing with the church, I will follow the instructions of my parents, my youth minister, and adult chaperones in order to promote the safety and wellbeing of myself and others.*

Looking quite contrite, the older brother asked, "How many times do we have to write it?"

"Glad you asked. I have a number in my head that is based on the number of times we had to write when I was in school. But I'm curious as to whether you all have a sense of remorse and justice. So here's what we're going to do... " (and I handed them each a piece of paper and a pen). John, you're going to write down how many times Luke has to write this sentence. And Luke, you're going to have to write how many times John has to write it. Whatever the other person says is how many times you're going to have to write it, and whatever you say is how many times the other person has to write it. But here's the catch: if your number is less than half of my number, I'm going to DOUBLE my number and that's how many times you'll have to write. Any questions?"

They reiterated the ground rules to me. They appeared both anxious and relieved by the hope that their parents wouldn't find out. I said, "OK. Go." With very little thought they both wrote on their papers and handed them to me. I looked at the numbers; older brother had assigned 10 to his little brother; little brother had assigned 25 to his brother. I announced the results. "But gee, I guess I really did grow up in a more strict generation than you all. When I was in school, and we got caught chewing gum, we had to write 500 times. (Granted, it was just "I will not chew gum in class," and I personally never got caught chewing gum because it never would have crossed my mind to put myself in such jeopardy.)

"Five hundred times!" they both gasped.

"Well, no. Remember, I said that if your number was less than half of mine it would be doubled. So it's 1000 times." Their faces looked so innocent and defeated I had to suppress a compassionate grin and the desire to say, "No, I'm just kidding, of course you don't have to write 1000 times." Before I could say anything, older brother— one of the nicest most compliant kids I've ever known said, "When do we have to have it done by?"

"Before the next event you want to attend." They nodded in stunned silence. "Now go eat," I said.

The next morning after church, their mother came up to me with an apprehensive smile. "Brad, the boys told me what they did. They told me they were very sorry and they were glad that you were willing not to tell their father. Since they confessed to me, do they still have to write the sentences?"

"No," I laughed. I was just trying to get them to tell you.

She laughed. "I thought that's what you were up to. Thank you."

*******

I had a reputation for being strict. While most of my drive was rooted in a desire to keep the young people safe, I must admit that I was often too harsh and that harshness had three main roots: my own rather strict upbringing; my jealousy of kids who got to do things I was afraid to do (like chewing gum in class); and my fear of the purse-strings-holding senior adults who might think I didn't have control. Early on in my work at one church, there was a curmudgeon who had ordained himself as the reporter of our unruly youth. In back to back to back encounters he had told me about the youth 1) turning all the hymnals in the sanctuary upside down, 2) changing the statistics board to indicate that the previous weeks' offering had been over $1,000,000, 3) discharging a fire extinguisher in the hallway, and 4) breaking a coffee maker in the Golden Years Sunday School classroom. After each of these events I had been thoroughly upbraided for "what [MY] youth had done." (When there was a problem, they were MY youth.) As one who was nearly paralyzed by a need for people's approval, I was terrified of people thinking I was not in control. It took far too long for me to learn that I was allowing irrational fears to control me. (The largest step I took in overcoming this came when I was seeing a therapist who suggested I read *The Feeling Good Handbook* by Dr. David Burns. I've often wished I had read this book BEFORE I spent so many years in ministry. As much training as Clinical Pastoral Education had offered to self-awareness, it had only made me aware that I had weaknesses without providing me the tools to debunk "cognitive distortions.") Thus, fearing that others would think I was not in control of the youth, I reactively strived to control them. Ironically, several years after the early criticism I received for letting the youth run roughshod over the building, I was telling that story to one of the young adults in the church. As it turned out, ALL of the incidents in question, from the inflated tithe report to the broken coffee pot had been done by her Sunday school class or one of the children of people who attended that class—children who were not in the youth group. Ouch.

Alas, for all my over-reactions, I did genuinely love "my kids" and was concerned for their safety. And eventually, one of my maneuvers did take effect. My first few trips to camp, I never got enough sleep due to youth refusing to go to bed at a reasonable hour. This was a safety issue because I was having to drive the van and needed to be well-rested. So, one year I decided to think of a "logical consequence" for keeping me awake. Since we always went to the beach on the last day of camp, I decided to use that as leverage. Before leaving for camp, I explained the safety issue of my needing to get enough sleep. "So, this year, for every minute past when I want to be asleep but am awake due to something you have done, I will DOUBLE that amount of time and you will sit out that amount of time at the beach. Please don't see if I mean this."

One person decided to be the guinea pig. On the last night of camp, I did a room check and found an empty room where a just-graduated-college-bound-high-school-senior had climbed out his window. I spent thirty minutes walking around campus looking for him. The next day he sat on a towel for one hour while the rest of us played in the surf. I never had another moment's problem at bedtime. Word got out. "Don't mess with Brad on rules; when he says 'I don't make many rules, but the ones I make, I enforce,' he means it.

Like the time I really meant it when I told Mary Beth that she wouldn't like what was going to happen if I saw her barefooted again. The very first time I had taken a church youth group on a trip, we had been at the beach house less than 10 minutes when a 7th grade boy nearly cut off his toe when he went wading in the Intercoastal Waterway and stepped on a broken mollusk shell of some variety. So, I was a little manic about shoes. Nothing dampens a trip like a long wait in the ER and stitches that impact both walking and swimming in the ocean.

On this trip we were tent camping at a campground in the Smoky Mountains. We were leading children's Bible activities in the mornings and family worship events in the late afternoons. One evening we were sitting around the fire and I noticed Mary Beth barefooted *again*. I made my ultimatum. A few minutes later she walked right by the fire in her unshod feet. "Mary Beth? Please go get your shoes and come back here and have a seat." While she went for her shoes, I went to my tent and got my rucksack. "What are you going to do?" Mary Beth asked with more giggle than trepidation. [Bad attention is better than no attention.]

I suppose I need to insert something at this point to help you know Mary a little better. Earlier that week, our whole group had inner-tubed down the nearby stream. We had gone through some mild whitewater and arrived in the valley near the campground where the stream became a lazy glide. We had linked into a blob of about 20 bodies and tubes drifting through the dense emerald canopy on our tranquil emerald conveyer.

Suddenly I noticed something destined to destroy our placid togetherness. About twenty yards ahead I noticed the bogey. With the calmness of a NASA announcement ("Houston, we have a problem."), I announced that everyone needed to remain calm. I wanted them to enjoy a close encounter with wildlife, wildlife that was now at 15 yards and closing. Its trajectory was taking in across our path at a speed that should have it well past by the time we arrived. We would be able to admire its grace from a comfortable distance. So I nonchalantly pointed out what was up ahead.

Come to find out, some people—like Mary Beth—have a lack of appreciation of a small garter snake es-ing its way across the surface of water.

It is extremely difficult to STAND on a moving inner-tube, especially while convulsing screams are rocking one's body. But Mary Beth almost did it. In fact, she stayed up longer than many professional bull riders stay on bulls named something like Grave Digger. Alas, Mary Beth fell off with a loud splash, and our friendly reptilian neighbor fairly flew across the water in the opposite direction as Mary Beth created doubt in all onlookers as to whether Jesus' walking on the water was really much of a miracle after all. Maybe he'd just seen a snake. Arriving back at the inner-tube, Mary Beth tried to stand on it again, only to wind up in a roiling mass of flailing that looked like an alligator wrestling match. The inner-tube won, but it was a valiant effort on Mary Beth's part.

Now she was in a tangle with me over her recalcitrance to wear proper foot gear. "Hold your foot up here," I said. She lifted up her now-shod foot. That shoe was not coming off for a while. With the deftness of an athletic trainer prepping a weak ankle and the speed of a rodeo calf roper, I duck taped Mary Beth's shoe to her ankle. She protested loudly during both applications, promising she would keep her shoes on, but I was undeterred. Unfortunately I did one of the wraps like I would have attached a cleat to a 300-pound offensive lineman. After a few minutes, Mary Beth complained that one of her ankles hurt. I looked, and, in point of fact, her lower calf was turning a little purplish blue at the perimeter of the tape. So, I took the tape off (riiiiiiip; "OOUUCH!") both feet (riiiiiip; "OUUUCH!"). But... no more problem with bare feet the rest of the trip.

\*\*\*\*\*\*

At least it had just been bare FEET with Mary Beth. With Jon-Jon, it was a bare prefrontal cortex (the part of the brain that provides impulse control).

I was driving into Atlanta, headed to a water park with a van load of mostly teenage boys, a smattering of girls (all sitting at the front), and one other adult chaperone who was riding shotgun. We were just getting into the white-knuckle section of the 3rd ring of hell that is the interstate southbound into Atlanta. I was leaning into the steering wheel, looking this way and that as vehicles zipped around like angry hornets. I reflexively glanced in the rearview mirror— briefly forgetting it would do no good with all the rows of heads between me and the back window. I couldn't see the vehicle behind me, but I did see Jon-Jon pressing his bared buttocks to one of the back... side (pardon the pun) windows.

"JON-JON!" I screamed.

Simultaneously I looked to my left and saw a woman with her lips pursed in disgust. She was looking just below where Jon-Jon's moon had been. I knew she was reading the bold-font name of our church that was emblazoned on the side of the van. I could see it in her eyes: *Baptists. Hmph.* To no avail, I mouthed "I'm sorry" as she passed, speeding in her Lexus. *Materialists. Hmph.*

One of the older boys later told me that Jon-Jon— an eighth grader— was just trying to get cool points with the older guys. He succeeded in some regard except that he got caught, leaving him with a net gain of "bless his heart." (Not that teenage boys say it like Southern women do, but they know the concept and think it even if they don't say it.)

But I was not going to bless his heart until I'd planted my Neil Armstrong boot on his moon. ("That's one small kick for a youth minister, one giant footprint to encourage development of a prefrontal lobe.") When we arrived at the water park, I drew Jon-Jon aside and— borrowing Mrs.

Finchum's line from the infamous high school ooga horn incident— said, "I am too mad to do anything right now." I let that sink in for a moment. "But while I'm cooling off— which may take the better part of an hour— you're going to sit out." I let him sit for a good long time and then told him I was still going to have to think about it.

About 30 minutes from home, Jon-Jon materialized in the shotgun seat. I knew what was coming. I toyed with him. "Did you have fun today?"

"Yeah. That was great."

I drove along in silence. He was going to have to say it and ask it.

"I'm sorry for what I did. That was really stupid." (Wait for it.) "Are you going to tell my parents?" (Bingo.)

"I admire your courage in apologizing. I'll tell you what. I won't tell your parents. But if anything like that ever happens again, I'll tell them about that AND this. Fair enough?"

"That's fair. Thanks, Brad."

I smiled.

Two years later his parents asked to see me after church. I knew what it would be about. I had a strict rule that after I made room assignments for camp, they could not be changed. I suspected that Jon-Jon's parents didn't like the roommate I had assigned— Ty, a poor inner city teen. Tough; they'd just have to deal with that.

The conversation started very humbly. It was headed where I thought it would be, but there was a card in their hand I had not anticipated.

"We know you don't change room assignments, and we understand that. You can't get into the game of swapping. It would be chaos. So we wouldn't ask if we didn't think it was necessary. Jon-Jon asked us to ask you for a reason we think is legitimate. He told us about the incident on the van a few years ago," Jon-Jon's father said with a chuckle. (Wow. This must be serious. I had underestimated Jon-Jon— or maybe just overlooked him growing up. He was smart enough to send his parents and to gain leverage with an unsolicited confession. He had my attention.) "Jon-Jon told us that last year at the annual youth retreat Ty brought a pornographic magazine and showed it to him." (I immediately remembered that Ty also was the person Jon-Jon had been trying to impress by dropping his pants on the van. I had to hand it to Jon-Jon; he was deftly connecting two events and leaving me little choice but to make an exception to my rule.) "Jon-Jon feels like he's very susceptible to Ty's influence and just wants to avoid problems."

"Consider it done." I reassigned Jon-Jon another roommate. Ty roomed with me and the other chaperone.

\*\*\*\*\*\*

"Can we go camping tonight?" Jimmy asked. He was a seventh grader. It was summer and we were about to start Sunday evening Bible study for a youth group that consisted of four regular attending boys representing the seventh, ninth, tenth, and twelfth grades. I was the youth minister in their rural church twenty-five miles from the urban seminary I was attending. The pastor, having his own home in the city, my wife and I lived in the parsonage and arms reach from one end of the church. In my basement I had a closet of camping gear.

"Tell you what. If you guys will give me 30 good minutes of Bible study, (I had worked hard preparing the lesson), we'll slip over to the house and get the gear together. Their eyes lit up. Jimmy's grandfather owned a huge farm with a fishing pond on the back forty of open pasture. There was a flat plain at the top of the hill by the pond. A perfect place for a bivouac.

We caught a string of brim before nightfall. (I made the mistake of staking them to the bank and leaving them in the pond to save for breakfast. The next morning I discovered that turtles eat fish. The string was as clean as dental floss.) After the sun set, flashlights emerged and we made several unsuccessful attempts at frog gigging in the thick grass of the bank. Eventually we were caught up in the ancient sacred ritual that binds us to humanity across the ages— gathered in a circle around a fire. I gazed into the embers, enraptured by the roiling of orange and red. "Mmm," I exhaled aloud, baiting my neophytes, a small school of curious brim, but my goal with this school was to lure them from the surface to new depths.

"What?" Ah, a taker.

"When I look into a fire, I feel connected to the very first humans."

"How's that?"

"Well, the world has changed a lot over the years. Fire is maybe the only thing that looks exactly the same to us as it did to the first humans."

"What do you mean?"

"Well, the landscape has changed because of volcanoes and things like that. The sky is a different color because of pollution. Plants look different after generations of cross pollination. But when we look into a fire, we are seeing the same thing that people have always seen."

There was a brief but surprisingly significant pause as they all looked into the fire.

"Tell us a ghost story, Brad!" Enough of the depths, back to the surface. Jimmy was leading the way.

"I don't know any ghost stories."

"Ah, come on!"

I was saved when someone passed gas. During the adolescent male bonding that ensued, and having been reminded of bodily functions, I ventured away from the fire circle and into the tall grass and the edge of darkness. I had my back to the cadre and was looking off into the distance as I... watered the grass. Suddenly I heard the distant sound of a chain saw. I scanned the next farm up on a hill about a quarter mile away. I saw a man—taking advantage of the cool of the night—using a street light mounted to the side of his barn to illuminate his cutting of firewood for winter. Inspiration comes in many forms.

I walked back to the fire circle and kept my voice high—and would talk virtually non-stop for the next minute.

"OK guys! I can't believe I forgot this, I just remembered that Mr. Brown told me a TRUE story about a ghost in these parts." (I sat down on a stump, while continuing to talk.) According to Mr. Brown, back when he was a young man, there was a Boy Scout troop that used to come camping out here. One night when they were out here, one of the boys had to go to the latrine that was built far enough from the campsite that it was out in the dark. He took a flashlight, but he turned it off while he was... you know... because he didn't want to be seen and he wanted to look at the stars. All of a sudden he heard the sound of a chain saw back at the campsite. He heard his fellow scouts and scoutmaster screaming. But the screams stopped one by one. The boy stayed low in the tall grass and ran as best he could back to the Brown's house and had them call the police. The police came and discovered the most horrific scene any of them had ever seen—even the ones who had been to war. Not a single survivor. And they say, on a quiet night, if you listen closely, you can still hear that chain saw."

Silence. Silence. (Come on!) And then, there it was.

Eight eyes nearly flew from their sockets. I'm fairly sure there was at least one mild case of incontinence.

Jimmy, the 7th grader who had begged for a ghost story... well, for the first time in my life, I saw someone scared stiff. He looked like a wax figure portraying someone who was trying to avoid detection by a boa constrictor.

Alan, rising high school senior and volunteer fire fighter, suddenly burst into laughter, fell on his large belly and started slapping the fertile earth and bellowing "That was AWESOME!"

The next morning I was frying bacon and the boys began coming one by one back to the fire circle. Jimmy sat down, wrapped in his sleeping bag. His eyes were flat and fixed in a catatonic stare.

"Jimmy? You OK, buddy?" I asked.

Only his lips moved. "I didn't sleep all night."

The other guys looked up from the hypnotic sizzling bacon just long enough to say with their eyes, *That was awesome. I didn't sleep well either at first.*

I think it was just a mild case of poetic justice for all the nights' sleep I've lost at the hands of rowdy youth. The adage says, "If youth knew and age could do." Since youth have such an abundance of energy that often wins at inflicting frustration or at flag football, it is fun to revel in the benefits of experience. For instance, I was once on a team of adult chaperones who were gathered on the field of Messy Olympics combat at a large summer camp. As we awaited the first round of competition of some relay race that involved baby oil and watermelons, our hormone-and-caffeine-infused opponents began chanting "We've got spirit, yes we do; we've got spirit, how 'bout YOU?"

"Huddle!" I yelled to my fellow adults. I made a quick suggestion, and several reached into their pockets.

We turned and faced our physically superior opponents. We raised our fists in defiance, dangling the symbols of our adult superiority and chanted back: "We've got van keys, yes we do; we've got van keys, how 'bout YOU!?"

Silence and flat stares from the youth. Victory was ours.

Of course victories often come after initial defeat. My first summer as a full time youth minister, the camp we would be attending had a "no electronic devices" rule. The rule sheet suggested that such devices could be used during travel to the camp as long as the youth minister took up the devices during camp. I wanted no part of that, so I just said, "No personal stereos may be brought. I will provide music over the van system."

We were not quite to the interstate when I saw two sets of headphones being worn. I pulled to the shoulder of the road.

"Gang, I don't make many rules, but the ones I make I enforce. I made it very clear that headphones were not to be brought on this trip." The 15-year-old boy on the back row glared at me as he removed his headphones.

Less than five miles later, with a merge onto the interstate almost imminent, I looked over my right shoulder to change lanes and saw a set of headphones on another young man— a student from another town, on the trip at the request of his grandparents with whom he apparently was in a month-long exile. He was sitting just outside the scope of the rearview mirror and apparently thought he was safe to be so brazen— being out of sight and a guest. The phrase "nip it in the bud" came to mind. I pulled over.

"OK. Maybe I didn't make myself clear. If I see another set of headphones, I will take the stereo away and will hand it to your parents when we get back to the parking lot at the end of the week." (I actually did that the next year.) Another glare and huff. But I didn't see anymore stereos.

(When comparing notes about that first summer, a colleague taught me another trick. She had every parent put a credit card number in a sealed envelope. She then told the youth that if there was a major breech of rules, she would put them on a plane or bus at their parents' expense. I implemented that a few years, and only had to threaten a bus trip one time— and it was after a young man's second trip to camp council and his PEERS said if they saw him again he'd be sent home. Kudos to the camp for setting up a peer system.)

The next summer, in the weeks leading up to camp, we were having a parents meeting. One of the mothers expressed concern that stereos were not going to be allowed on the trip. "It's a 10-hour drive," she said. "They need something to do."

I smiled and asked to be excused for a moment. I walked to my office, retrieved a tightly folded piece of notebook paper, and returned to the conference room.

"Last Wednesday night after youth Bible study, I found this lying in the floor. This is in the handwriting of one of our youth. These are the lyrics of a song this person had written down." Without batting an eye, I read the words verbatim— including the words fu@#, bi@#$, and nigg@# and a series of crystal clear vulgar descriptions of various sex acts.

"Now. Here's the deal. If you want the kids to bring their CD players, I won't be able to hear what they are listening to, and they WILL share their personal CDs, and some of our students WILL be listening to this kind of music. One question I have is: do you want your child sitting next to someone who is listening to this kind of thing." (I could see in the eyes of the parents that I had already won them over, but I pressed on.) I consider our trip to camp to be a spiritual pilgrimage, and I want them in a mindset for that. I will have music that we can all listen to. And it they get bored they can learn to talk to each other.

To her credit, the mother who had so adamantly argued for personal stereos immediately spoke up. "You've convinced me. I say, 'No stereos.'"

A few years later, we were at the same camp— a camp that gave an "honor camper of the day award" to a student from each of about 10 groups of 25 students representing a mix from all the churches in attendance. One day, a youth member from my group was the honor camper in every single group. At the end of the week, a chaperone from another church approached me and asked me my secret. "About what?" I asked. He then said, "I've noticed that youth from your church contribute to discussion. And I notice that each night when we have church group devotions, when everyone else finishes and is running around, your group is still talking. How do you get them to open up?"

"Two things," I said. "First, we meet once a week and do something we call 'SOS— for Sharing our Stories.' We shut the door and I tell them, 'What is said in here, stays in here, and we just talk— no structure other than my guiding the conversation a little. Second, I don't let them bring stereos on trips like this. They complained about it when I first came, but now they wouldn't have it any other way. They've learned to talk to each other."

Of course there are pitfalls to having youth talk to each other. My philosophy has been that they are going to talk anyway; it's better for them to have adult guidance in doing it. But one lesson I learned the hard way was the pitfall of something supposedly as innocuous as the ritual of sharing prayer requests.

We had a new boy in the youth group. Chris's father was the new principal at the middle school most of the group attended. (The new principal was seen as an unwelcome outsider after the very popular previous principal had been moved to another school.) Chris was a bit bookish and trying a bit too hard to win the affection of girls who weren't interested and the admiration of fellow males who were genuinely trying to tolerate his very disingenuous efforts to talk smack about sports teams.

One Wednesday evening at youth Bible study we were following our usual routine of starting with prayer. To promote praise, I would roll a die from the game Scattergories— a 26-sided die with all the letters of the alphabet. Whatever letter showed, the students would call out words starting with that letter that described a quality of God. Then I'd open the floor for things folks were thankful for or concerned about. On this occasion, the first person said, "I appreciate if you all would pray for me because grade cards came out today, and my parents are going to kill me." A hand shot up— the hand of a young woman with a despairing face. "Me, too. I'm probably going to be grounded for a month." Another hand shot up; another solemn face. "Me, too. I haven't showed my parents my report card yet." (Only the most naïve person would miss the fact the person was considering forging the required signature.) Three more similar "requests" were made. Then Chris raised his hand. "I have something I'm thankful for." He paused. I nodded for him to continue— one of the costliest nods of my life. "I was really nervous about coming to a new school— you know, moving here just before school started and trying to unpack and adjust to all this new stuff. I was really worried about how I would do, so I'm really thankful that I got straight A's."

When— later in my office— I gently began to confront Chris about his less than sensitive timing, I hadn't even finished my sentence when he started nodding that he knew he had goofed. But it was too late. My youth group, that had never had more than a mild tiff, broke out into full scale civil war. It went on for a few months, with the trouble between youth spreading to tension between their parents.

The conflict went on until a weekend retreat that coincided with my birthday. One of the older youth asked me what I got for my birthday and it gave me an idea. Before loading the van to leave, I called four of the natural leaders into a room. "I got some cool stuff for my birthday, but there is one thing that I want more than anything— and it doesn't cost a dime." I paused for effect. "This group will do whatever you all do. What I want for my birthday— more than anything— is for you all to pretend you like Chris." I could see the immediate reluctance on their faces. One of the guys literally sighed. "I know he gets on your nerves, but you may be surprised what will happen if you all give him some positive attention. If he tells a corny joke, I want you all to laugh like you would if Tyler had told it. If he wants a high five, you give it and say, 'You da man.'" I paused again. "I love you folks, and I know you love me too. I would greatly appreciate this gift." They did it. On the last night of the retreat we had one of the most powerful reconciliations I have ever seen.

Injury and healing. Typically, the church is a place to promote spiritual and emotional healing. If we do assist in physical healing, it usually is at a hospital or clinic we sponsor. We certainly don't want to *create* the need for healing— of any kind, though we often do. Hippocrates' rule for physicians is a good rule for all professions: "first do no harm." That's why youth ministers often dread lock-ins: they are a cauldron of hormones and unbridled energy in which folks with undeveloped frontal lobes are placed under the charge of adult chaperones whose own frontal lobes have been dulled by having been at work all day.

I was in the fellowship hall monitoring the youth who had been captured and were being held in "jail" by "Roman soldiers" in a game called underground church. It was about 3:00 in the morning. A girl ran into to the room and yelled, "Brad, Jonathan is hurt." Her face let me know this was no joke. She turned, gesturing for me to follow. As I ran after her, I began trying to process that contradiction in the statement "Jonathan is hurt." JONATHAN did not GET hurt. If he had been hit by a slow-moving car, there likely would be more damage to the car. But as I turned down the darkened hallway, I saw JONATHAN's silhouette prostrate face up at the far end of the hall. There was enough light that as I approached I saw a trail of blood leading to Jonathan's head. His eyes were dazed and fixed. I told him to lie still— the easiest instruction he ever had to follow— and I tried to find the hole from which the blood was coming. Then I noticed that the blood drops got bigger as they went AWAY from Jonathan. I told Jennifer to stay with Jonathan, and I followed the trail that I now noticed led to the nearest men's room. I opened the door and saw Jonathan's older brother, Allan, standing before a sink that was completely coated in blood. Allan had his hand over his nose. I walked over beside him and, addressing him in the mirror, said, "Let me see." He removed his hand. His nose— which had previously been nicely centered— was now under his left eye.

As it turns out, Jonathan had been running down the far hallway and made the sharp right turn onto the main hall, only to see some of his opponents at the other end. He stopped on a dime and turned to retreat. Allan had come full speed around the corner and had plowed his nose into his brother's infamously hard head.

Just before noon, Allan was taken into surgery. Jonathan was fine.

I've been staring at the blinking cursor for quite a while, wondering how to end this chapter. I have this image of standing before a twelve-step recovery group saying, "Hi, I'm Brad, I like to host youth lock-ins," and the group saying "Hi, Brad."

**Questions for Reflection**

1) Did you read the footnote on p. 106? It describes a family secret, the discovery of which was simultaneous one of the most traumatic and liberating of my life, yet in this book it was presented in a footnote. What incidents in your life may be the small spark in the piston that is driving much of your public persona and activities?

2) Pick one or more of the crises in this chapter and describe advance precautions that might have prevented the problem.

# CHAPTER 9

## Thou Shalt Not "Play Tennis" But with Thine Own Partner

"IF I WERE WILLING TO COMMIT ADULTERY, all I would need for it to happen in the hospital is ten minutes and an empty room." My fellow ministerial students and I gazed at our seminary instructor in awkward silence. He paused for effect. "I don't know about female chaplains, but a male chaplain would have no problem getting sex in a hospital. Because there tend to be lots of females in hospitals. And the more females there are, the more likely it is that one is lonely. And what characteristics do most women find attractive? They are attracted to men who are caring, gentle, kind, compassionate, and good listeners. Characteristics usually found in what employees in the hospital? Chaplains."

Many persons opposed to women preaching say it is because men, being more prone to visual arousal, would be too likely to be... distracted... by a female preacher. By the same logic, maybe male preachers should avoid preaching and ministering in a way that is caring, gentle, kind, compassionate, and indicative of good listening, since that supposedly promotes attraction by females. Some argue men should not counsel women—especially alone. But what if you're a male counseling with a couple and the woman makes a pass at you with her husband sitting right beside her? At least it sounded to me like a pass.

She was gorgeous. Athletic. Sweet. Friendly. Bubbly. Fresh. Clean. Nubile. Her makeup was just right—she didn't need any—just used enough to say "I like to get dolled up." And she made assertive eye contact with her glowing eyes. In short, she was just like my wife. Except for the ways she wasn't like my wife. She likely would not listen to National Public Radio with me. She would never be able to go camping without a hair dryer to care for that thick, cascading ebony hair. And she preferred a night out drinking with the gal pals to spending more time with her man. But then again, she was *gorgeous. Athletic. Sweet. Friendly. Bubbly. Fresh. Clean. Nubile. Her makeup was just right— she didn't need any— just used enough to say "I like to get dolled up." And she made assertive eye contact with her glowing eyes.*

She had even bobbed her head cutely when she had said it. And raised her eyebrows just so. And smiled perfectly.

Did she really just say that? With her fiancé sitting *right there* beside her? Her fiancé! Her tubby, acne-scarred, struggled-to-pass-the-G.E.D. fiancé! What was *she* doing with *him*? "*She* doing with *him*?" What was *he*, a really nice guy, doing with *her*, Little-Miss-You'll-Never- Be- Able-to-Make-Me-Happy. Poor schmuck!! He wouldn't even care if I "played tennis" with her, as long as she came back to his court eventually.

Playing tennis. That's what started it. We were in our fourth premarital counseling session at a church-based counseling center where I was doing my internship. We had been talking about how couples don't always like the same activities and need to respect one another's tastes. "For instance," I had said. "I love to play tennis. My wife *hates* tennis. She's a perfectionist, and because she can't play tennis extremely well, she doesn't want to play at all. For the longest time that bugged me. But I finally learned that she didn't have to play tennis for me to love her. I could find somebody else to play tennis with. So I . . ."

"I'll play tennis with you!" my female client said perkily.

I stared blankly. I had been about to say that I started playing tennis with an old buddy from high school.

"Really," she said, looking over at her fiancé, nodding for his approval. "I love to play tennis, and Junior doesn't like anything that doesn't involve an engine or a remote." Junior smirked and nodded his consent.

*My gosh. He really is oblivious! He doesn't know what she's doing when she's out with the girls, and he wouldn't care if she and I "played tennis."*

I don't remember anything else about the content of the rest of the session. She was gorgeous. Athletic. Sweet. Friendly. Bubbly. Fresh. Clean. Nubile. Her makeup was just right— she didn't need any— just used enough to say "I like to get dolled up." And she made assertive eye contact with her glowing eyes. In short, my client was just like my wife. Except for the ways she wasn't like my wife. My client had not had two miscarriages and spent the last two years in depression. My client wasn't smiling just because she was out in public; my client was really happy. She was vivacious; she looked interested in *me*. She was willing to play tennis with *me*. *And* she was gorgeous, athletic, sweet, friendly, bubbly, fresh, clean, and nubile, with just-so eye shadow and eyeliner on her assertive, glowing eyes, and shimmering gloss on her pinkened pouty lips. Venus De Milo... but with arms emerging from a well-curved, sweater vest. Capri pants revealed a chiseled calf muscle that had been toasted golden brown on a beach towel in her back yard. *She takes the time to lie in the sun and pamper herself.* Smooth skin from hot wax. *She is willing to take the pain to look her best.* And her husband-to-be is paying for all her primping. I could "play tennis" with her on his nickel. What a bargain!

*But he's paying me to help them. What am I thinking!? I need to... Oh my gosh, her neck is so pretty.*

Fortunately, my heart was racing not merely from attraction; most of the excess pulse rate was from fear. I still had the presence of mind to be scared of the end results of *pursuing* the thoughts I was having. In fact, as a hospital chaplain I had learned to nurture that fear rather than to interpret it as weakness. Shortly after I had been told how easy it would be for a chaplain to exploit the role of compassionate listener, I had come face to face with the reality, face to face with a blushing female nurse.

I was at a nurses' station on one of my regular units, standing at the counter carrying on some cheerful banter with two female nurses working on charts at the desk on the other side of the counter. I had worked closely with both of them and respected them both not only as professionals but as fellow Christians who genuinely used nursing to minister to their patients with Christ-like compassion. As I turned to walk away, one of the nurses said something. I thought she was speaking to me and that I had not heard her. I stopped and turned back around. "What was that, Ruth?" I asked.

"Oh, nothing," she said. "I was talking to Naomi."

Naomi snorted. "She said you're… ." Naomi had stopped when Ruth backhanded her fairly hard on the arm.

Blushing, Ruth looked at me. I could see her doing some quick mental calculus. She came to the conclusion she would rather confess than leave me thinking she might have said something unkind. "I said, 'You're… ." Her voice trailed off.

"What?"

Now embarrassed and frustrated she blurted with an emphatic whisper, "*I said, 'You're such a hunk.*" She bobbed her head and raised her eyebrows to say *There, I said it; can we move along now?* and went back to charting. Naomi shook her head smiling and did the same.

I walked away in shock. Not since eighth grade had anyone called me a hunk. And that was Roberta Hornrim, the slightly odd gal who wrote it in my annual. "Since you changed your part, you've become a hunk," she wrote in big bubble letters, referring to my having gone from the on-the-side part to the very late 1970's middle-parted wings coiffure. Anybody who thought I was a hunk had to be weird. I weighed 90 pounds. I was great at hide-and-go-seek because I could hide behind a table leg.

But Ruth wasn't weird. She wasn't exactly a hottie, but she wasn't weird. She was single and searching. I was married but very insecure, convinced that I was still an ugly duckling, but Ruth was making me feel like a swan, no... an eagle.

"I'm so scared of committing adultery," I told my fellow chaplains in our next group meeting after my encounter with Ruth. "I spend so much time worrying about being unfaithful to my wife. I'm really not that attracted to Ruth. What if somebody I was attracted to said something like that. What would I do? I mean I'm scared to death that I don't have the will power to resist that kind of temptation."

One of my supervisors spoke up. "You sound like you think your fear is a bad thing."

I shrugged as if to say, *isn't it?*

"Brad, the day you stop being scared of the capacity to commit adultery is the day you need to worry."

Everyone stared at me. I let that sink in. It was OK to be scared. In fact, I *needed* to be scared. It was fear of being burned that would keep me away from the fire.

Now here I sat in a counseling session, and the fire on the other side of the room looked so warm and inviting. It danced in my eyes. It smelled of a lush tropical beach. It sizzled and crackled the taunting sounds of the forbidden, sounds I fondly recalled from high school and college.

Even after the bride and groom left the room, the fire lingered. And then it began to spread. I needed help putting it out. I searched the counseling center. All my colleagues had left. I called my supervisor; no answer. I called Jonathan, a trusted colleague I knew working at another counseling center.

"Got a minute?"

"Yeah, what's up?"

"I need to get something off my chest." I searched for the words. "I know that it's dangerous to keep secrets. So I just need to get this out, because I can't go home feeling like I feel right now," meaning I couldn't face my wife.  I told him about my client, about her invitation to play tennis, about her other similarities with the tennis star Anna Kournikova, and about my attraction to more than her tennis abilities. "I feel like such scum. I mean part of me is angry and feeling lonely because Connie has been having such a hard time. She just hasn't been herself since the miscarriages. But for crying out loud, there have been many times when I've been out of it, and she has been so encouraging and supportive of me. I'm very aware that the very things I find attractive about this gal are the things I find attractive about Connie. We as human beings can be so greedy, and right now I'm being very greedy. And like I said, I just needed to say this out loud, so that I could feel clean before I go home and be able to make eye contact."

Jonathan told me he thought I was wise to talk to someone and reminded me that there was nothing wrong with feeling attraction, just acting on it. Then he said, "Since you will continue working with this client, what do you think about telling your supervisor about this?"

"Oh, as soon as I get the chance."

"Good. And Brad?"

"Yeah."

"If I ever ask you to play tennis, I'm only… ."

"Shut up, Jonathan."

A few days after our last session, my "Anna-Kournikova-client" called. She was sobbing.

"Brad? … You're an ordained minister aren't you?"

"Yes."

"You can perform weddings?"

"Yes."

"Junior and I just found out that our minister was in a bad car accident. He's going to make it, but he's in the hospital. Our wedding rehearsal is in five hours. Is there any possibility you could do our wedding?"

I gulped silently. "Gee, Anna, I certainly want to do everything I can to help. My gut is to say yes, and if I can I will, but I need to check with my supervisor first about legalities and things like that. I can't imagine that it would be a problem, but our oversight agency has a lengthy list of ethics rules about keeping counseling relationships separated from other relationships. Let me make a phone call and get back to you. But know this, if I can't do it for some reason, I have lots of connections, and I'll help you find someone who can."

I used the phone call to my supervisor to compose myself. I didn't really believe there would be a problem with my performing a client's wedding, particularly given the circumstances. I did, however, really believe that I did not want to see the bride in some low-cut wedding dress. It's distracting enough to be standing on a dais looking down at a bride, seeing areas maybe better reserved for her groom and the honeymoon. It's bad enough to try to feel holy when the bride bulging from her corseted gown is *not* someone you have felt was flirting with you. How would I handle it now? Would people see the attraction in my eyes?

Fortunately, her gown turned out to be very conservative, with a bejeweled and sequined collar all the way up her neck. I found myself distracted not by the beauty of the bride but by unusually large number of apparently lesbian couples attending the wedding. One in particular had a— what was it?— sly, mysterious grin toward the bride.

I wasn't sure about this supposition at the rehearsal dinner. But at the wedding, as I stood at the front of the sanctuary, looking across the congregation, it became very clear. For this Bible Belt town, there was a higher than usual number of lesbian couples at this wedding. At least they fit the stereotype, as when one of the women raised a camera that had rainbow bars embroidered on her camera strap.

*Oh my gosh! Junior said his biggest frustration was that his bride-to-be seemed to prefer bar hopping with the gals to being with him. I thought it was strange at the time. Usually it's the woman complaining about the man being out with the guys. So why does this bride spend so much time out with her gal pals? Is it that she also is a lesbian? Just because so many of her friends are doesn't mean she is. Or maybe she's bisexual. At the very least, even if she is heterosexual, maybe Junior wonders if she's gay. And I missed it. Was I so caught up in my heterosexual attraction to Anna that I didn't even consider the fact that she might be gay? How many times have I heard of people getting married thinking it would dispel their homosexual feelings? Is that what's going on here? Am I about to perform a wedding for someone who is getting married out of a need to change something about herself rather than out of a desire to love someone for the rest of her life? When I ask if there are any objections to this wedding proceeding, should I, myself, object?* "If you all will excuse us, I need to have a word with the bride and groom out in the hallway just a moment. ... Anna, just for the record, are you a lesbian?" *No, I can't do that. Oh my gosh! I can't believe I didn't trust my gut. I knew something seemed strange about Junior's accusation about her spending more time out with her gal pals than with him. He couldn't bring himself to tell me he wondered if Anna were gay. And now that* I'm *wondering if she's gay, I'm wondering if she's marrying this taciturn guy because he's the closest thing she can get to a woman and still be with a man. And... wait a second, if she is gay, what does that say about her supposed attraction to* me? *OK, if she is gay, it doesn't mean I'm effeminate if she found me attractive. Maybe she's bisexual. But even if she's not gay, I blew it by not helping Junior put the issue to rest in his mind. And maybe I missed it because I was arrogantly thinking that she was wasting her beauty on him, that she really wanted to play tennis with* me.

The organist began to play the march. The mother of the bride led the congregation to stand. *Oh, God, help me.*

I nearly ended this essay with the preceding sentence. Then I realized another segment needed to be told.

When we were in seminary, Connie was working as a teaching assistant for one of our professors. One day he looked up from his work and said, "Connie, you need to fail at something." She looked at him and said, "O... K."

It was her fear of failure that had impeded her willingness to play tennis with me. She was paranoid about spectators laughing at her. She needed to be in control. And sometimes the only way to learn how not to be in control is not to have any choice. Now, I'm *not* saying God inflicts infertility to teach us a lesson, but I do believe that out of our personal hurts, God can teach us. In our case, three years of miscarriages and infertility created a situation completely beyond Connie's control. It forced her to face imperfection and helped me be less self-centered. Although she did nothing to cause her infertility and miscarriages, Connie felt like a failure. She cried a lot.

Then suddenly she was pregnant. The pregnancy was exciting and fine until the sixth month. At five months she had gone to Chile on a church mission trip. Her doctor had cleared it saying, "The fifth month is the best time to travel, and I have a good friend who is an obstetrician in the city where you are going." But shortly after getting back, Connie became sick. Her doctor suggested she had picked up giardia from the water in Chile. The first stool sample needed for accurate diagnosis was improperly shipped to the lab. The second frozen sample thawed when the flight carrying it to the lab was grounded after the terrorist attacks in New

York and Washington, D.C. on September 11, 2001. After two months and the third botched sample, this one the lab's fault again, I threw a temper tantrum that got the attention of the head of laboratory services. He was on the verge of personally driving the sample to Minnesota. Since it was going to take a week to get the results *after* they were shipped, the doctor decided to go ahead and treat Connie for giardia. The treatment didn't help. It didn't help because as it turned out, she didn't have giardia. As it turned out, as soon as our son was born, the extreme nausea and dizziness went away. Apparently she had had toxemia from the weight of the baby pinching her colon closed.

Our son came in November. The following May we were leaving to go on vacation to Lake Junaluska, a Methodist retreat center in the mountains near Asheville, North Carolina. I had the van packed, and we were making our last check of the packing list. Connie picked up the brochure from the retreat center. "This says they have tennis courts. You didn't pack the tennis rackets," she said with a teasing smile.

I played along. "They're still in off-season. There probably won't be anybody there to play with."

"I'll play tennis with you," she said with a flirting flick of her eyebrows.

And she did. Quite well as a matter of fact. We had the place almost completely to ourselves. On the last morning when we were packing, Connie said, "I hate to leave. After we check out, could we play tennis one more time?" I smiled. We did.

But as we were playing, busloads of people began arriving for the first day of the summer season. I worried Connie might get self-conscious. "You want to leave?" She made a face to say *are you crazy, I'm still on vacation.*

Our daughter, Delyn, was playing on the playground equipment immediately beside the tennis courts. Our infant son had been asleep in an infant carrier in the shaded corner of the court for over an hour. We were having the time of our lives. Connie went to collect a stray ball. I looked over at our daughter, thankful that she could play so well in solitude. I smiled, remembering the night before. We had sat on a hillside beneath the center's landmark lighted cross, looking down on the lake twinkling the reflected lights of cabins on the bank. We looked at the lights and the cross through the wooden kaleidoscope Delyn had gotten the day before for her sixth birthday. Before we went back to the cabin, we prayed together. Delyn said, "Thank you, God, that we got to come to Lake Junaluska." Tears had come to my eyes, thankful that my daughter was grateful for an inexpensive, no frills cabin in lieu of Disney World. Now, I surveyed my family: my precious daughter stretching her imagination on a set of monkey bars; my son sleeping peacefully; and my wife, full of spunk, charging the net and smoking me on a slam right at my feet.

As I went to retrieve the ball I saw a man and boy standing near the fence watching us. The boy was about the age of my daughter. I bobbed my head forward and waved to the man in greeting as I bent down to pick up the ball. Straight-faced he bobbed his back. As I turned to walk back, they turned to walk toward the lake. I heard the man say, "I wish your mother and I could do that."

"Why can't you?" the little boy asked.

With disdainful venom dripping from his voice the man said, "Because we're always with *you*."

I wanted to throw my racket at the man. My anger kept me from thinking to do what I wish I had done. I wish I had said, "Sir! Excuse me. I couldn't help but overhear what you said. Our daughter is right there. We'll be glad to watch the kids play and let you and your wife use our rackets."

I'd be willing to bet that if I had said that, he would have said, "No, that's OK. Actually, my wife doesn't play tennis. I've just wanted to."

Dealing with these kinds of situations is not something we spent much time discussing in seminary or college. (That's part of the reason I'm writing this book.) but there is one distinct exception where my training was very pragmatic. My undergraduate program had me well prepared for seminary. I took an advanced placement test and tested out of introduction to Old Testament. I did not, however, pass the New Testament section. But my college New Testament professor (who was a retired pastor teaching as an adjunct) did have me well prepared for a test of a different kind.

One day in class, Dr. Horton said, "Now all you preacher boys listen up. When you go out on visitation, you make sure you take along one other man or two women. Do not put yourself in the position to be alone with a woman. When I was pastor in New York City, you would not believe what women showed up at the door dressed in. One time I went to visit a woman at her apartment at her request. I took two women from the church with me. When I knocked on the door the two women were standing to the left of the door. When the woman inside opened the door, she was standing there in a negligee. She started to say 'Hiiii, pastor,', but she only made it as far as 'Hii' when she saw the other two women. Then she said, "Oh goodness, I wasn't expecting you this soon. I thought you were.... Wait here and let me go get something else on.'"

Years later I was serving at a church where we decided to have a rummage sale to raise money for summer camp. Our advertising worked very well and we were deluged with an army of bargain hunters. (Two of them nearly came to blows in a dispute over a *nativity scene*. One had picked up a wise man; the other had picked up Jesus. I would have thrown the whole mangled set into the trash. One of the women finally conceded just about the time I was going to take a sword and cut all the pieces in two.) About two hours into the chaos, I was summoned to the office for a phone call. A woman informed me that the electric organ she had purchased for $50 had worked just fine at the church, but when she got it home it didn't work at all. Rather than lug it back to the church, she wanted to know if I would come try to fix it. I told her I would, and that I would bring $50 in case I couldn't. Walking down the hall, I saw Allen. Perfect.

"Allen, we got a call from a woman who needs to have an item repaired or returned. Just in case I can't fix it, I need a truck. Can you drive me?" He tossed me his keys and said, "Just take it." I caught the keys and headed for the parking lot. It took just two steps before the ghost of Dr. Horton said, "Whoa, preacher boy."

"Hey, Allen. Just in case I need help carrying it, why don't you come with me?" We pulled into the woman's driveway less than 10 minutes after she called. Approaching the modest 1940s home, I saw a piece of paper taped to the front door. "I'm in the back yard. Come on around!" Walking around the house, I looked at Allen and said, "I'm going to die if she's lying out back in a bikini."

I carefully rounded the corner. Allen was concealed by a hydrangea. There she lay on a beach chair, golden brown, eyes closed, wearing a bikini made from— as they say— about as much cotton as might be found in an aspirin bottle.

"Excuse me," I called. She sat up, beamed a smile and...

Allen stepped fully into the back yard. Here smile vanished. "Oh goodness! I didn't think you'd get here so fast." (*Oh, I guess that's why you left a note on the door.*) "Let me go inside and get something on. I'll meet you at the front."

Allen and I started back toward the front. As soon as we were beside the house, he slumped over against the wall. "What?" I asked.

Shaking his head and smiling in disbelief, Allen said, "How did you know?"

"Because in the spring of 1985, I had Dr. Jim Horton for New Testament."

**Questions for Reflection**

1) How do you respond to the assertion that attraction is not wrong? Where is the line between attraction and lust?

2) Jesus said that to lust is the same as committing adultery. Accepting this, what may be the danger of equating attraction with lust?

3) What are proactive steps to deal with attraction?

4) What are some steps that should be avoided? (i.e., Some might feel the need to clear the air by talking to the person for whom they feel the attraction. How might this backfire?)

5) The college professor suggested that "preacher boys" take someone with them on visitation. Would the same rule apply to females serving in ministerial positions? What about other professions besides ministry? (When I worked for UPS as a driver helper one Christmas, each of the drivers with whom I worked said they had customers on their routes who seemed to order packages just to get the delivery worker to come to the door where they were met with seductive clothing and sultry eyes.) What precautions could be carried out if companions are not possible?

6) At the end of the wedding anecdote, one reviewer wrote, "This is scary." At this point the same reviewer wrote: "Dude, I thought you'd at least tell us how things turned out at the wedding in your Qs, but no! You'll have frustrated readers if you don't tell!!!! In fact, I may have to call you right now!" How do you feel right now when I ask, "What would you have done?" (without telling you what I did)?

## CHAPTER 10

### Through the Perilous Fight

"THE WEST VIRGINIA BEING OUT OF PLACE in formation saved all our lives."

The 70-year-old World War II veteran in the bed in front of me had been blown six feet in the air by the first bomb to fall at Pearl Harbor. He was reclining then, too— reading a paper on the deck of the U.S.S. Tennessee. He had stared down the barrel of death 52 years before. Then, he had been surrounded by others. Now, on the eve of open heart surgery, Mr. Fortune was alone.

I was the on-call chaplain, so I was making pre-surgical visits to everyone having surgery the next morning. It was dark outside beyond the window, a misty snow falling past the illuminated windows across the street. Mr. Fortune's wife had left to go home before the roads got bad. In the course of our conversation he mentioned being in the navy during World War II.

Having been instilled as a child with a respect for veterans, I tended to show more interest than most people my age, so, on a number of occasions I have heard stories men have "never told [their] own children." I suppose my interest was partially prompted by my having never known my paternal grandfather, who died seven months before my father was born. My grandfather died in February, Dad was born in August, and the attack on Pearl Harbor happened in December. The oldest of Dad's eight brothers was immediately drafted. The second oldest, driven by poverty and propaganda, harassed my grandmother until she signed a waiver for him to volunteer at age 17. Even before Tom Brokaw called them *The Greatest Generation*, I was intrigued with their stories.

"I joined up on the buddy plan with my best friend," Mr. Fortune said with a smile. "And low and behold we actually were assigned to the same boat. You know you hear all the time about guys who sign up on the buddy plan and never see each other again. And we were among the few Tennesseans assigned to the Tennessee." He looked out across the sea of time, now wider than the Pacific ocean, but close enough to put his feet in the still bloodied water.

"During the last maneuvers before the attack, we were coming back into The Harbor. We were supposed to enter in the order we were to be docked. But the harbor master told the West Virginia they were out of position and to circle back around. When they circled back around that put us on the Tennessee going in second behind the Oklahoma. That meant that we ended up mooring next to the dock and the West Virginia mooring beside us. Usually it was the other way around. So, boy, were we upset. See, it was favorable to be moored on the outside. That way you got the breeze. Now the West Virginia was blocking our breeze." Mr. Fortune began falling more and more into a trance with each passing sentence. "If you were moored next to the dock on your starboard, the other ship on your port blocked the breeze. So, oh did we ever raise a ruckus. We fussed and fumed something fierce." He glanced at me ever so slightly, shook his head and returned to the hypnotic stare of survivor's guilt.

"The West Virginia being out of place in formation saved all our lives. They ended up taking the torpedoes that would have hit us. The Arizona was moored at our stern, the Oklahoma at our bow, and the dock was to our starboard, so we were shielded on all four sides." Mr. Fortune paused. "It took two weeks for us to blast our way out of there. Then we limped back to San Diego for repairs."

I told that story one day in a church sanctuary. I was talking to the widow of a World War II veteran. Her husband, a close friend of mine and political debate sparring partner, had died a few months before. On December 6, 1941 they had become Mr. and Mrs. Raymond Brass and spent their second night as husband and wife listening to the radio in a hotel lobby. Then Ray had left for Europe for four years. He had parachuted into Normandy on D-day, gotten separated from his platoon behind enemy lines, and spent three days hiding from Nazis. He made it back to his company, having recorded the coordinates of a German bunker, and got the Bronze Star. Virginia kept the medal in a frame next to Ray's picture on her bedside table.

She didn't know why I had asked her to meet with me, much less why in the sanctuary. It was a spur of the moment invitation when I had seen her doing some work setting up her Sunday school room as was her custom on Thursdays.

We sat side saddle, facing each other on the second pew. I told her I was frustrated about a situation going on in the youth group. I was getting hit from both sides over an unpopular decision and course of action. Two years before, in 1997, I had used the word *context* during a youth Bible study. I stopped to make sure they understood the meaning of *context*. The younger ones didn't; I was already concerned. This was a group of 20 students ranging from 8th to 12th grade, and, other than two or three high school seniors, I was getting blank stares over the word *context*. "OK, for instance: I have a friend who was born in 1941 and didn't meet his father until he was five years old. Based on your knowledge of world events, what is the probable *context* that would explain that?" Blank stares. "Come on you all. What major world event was taking place in the world from 1941 to roughly 1945?" An eighth grade girl ventured, "Columbus discovered America?"

I nearly cried.

The next day I was having lunch at one of the several high schools represented in my youth group. I was eating with a bright senior who had been in the study the night before. I reasoned to myself that maybe dates were not as important as the *meaning* of history. So I asked him, "What can you tell me about Adolf Hitler?"

He thought for a moment. "I don't know. We talked about him in history one time. I think he did some stuff that scared a lot of people."

When I told this part of the story in the sanctuary, Virginia gasped and shook her head in disgust and despair.

"What have we done wrong, Brad? You know what they say about failing to learn from history! What are we going to do?"

"Well, I'll tell you what I did. First I wrote a three-page letter to the superintendent of schools and told that story. I made some suggestions for curriculum. But I said I wasn't writing to blame the schools. I was going to take responsibility, too. And I did. I spent the next year researching the major historical events of the Twentieth Century: Prohibition, the wars, civil rights, nuclear arms, the space race.... Then I created a series of Bible studies entitled *Christians' Contribution and Reactions to the Major Historical Events of the Twentieth Century.* I put a *lot* of work into it. I tried really hard to make it exciting for the youth. Like to study the issue of the Apocalypse, I got audio clips from Orson Well's *War of the Worlds* and talked about all that hullabaloo. In fact, I had Ray come and talk about his experience in the war when we talked about World War II."

Virginia smiled sadly. "I know."

I was afraid I might have hit too close to a nerve for Virginia. Ray had been dead less than 3 months and his visit with the youth had come just a few weeks before his final bout with liver cancer.

"The youth will never forget *that* night," I said.

One of the brighter boys had boldly asked Ray, "How do you reconcile going to war and killing with the commandment 'Thou shalt not kill'?" The question had not been asked in malice and Ray did not take it that way. He had somberly pursed his lips and with tears in his eyes said, "I've wrestled with that every day for the last 60 years."

I continued building my case with Virginia in earnest: "The thing is, I know the youth have been getting a lot out of this series. And I've tried to make it not only informative but exciting. But I'm *still* getting slammed with criticism. I suppose I could handle it if it were just the kids. I mean, you expect kids to complain about eating vegetables, even if they know there will be ice cream for dessert. But we as adults have an obligation not only to give kids what they want, but what they need."

"That's *right*," Virginia agreed, emphatically nodding her head.

"The thing is, now I've got some parents almost demanding that I stop the series. One mother told me she had told her daughter she didn't have to go to youth Bible study. She told me, 'The kids have been at school all day on Wednesday; they don't need another history lesson.'" Virginia grimaced, nonplussed. "A father of another youth member told me I ought to be teaching the Bible, not history. He didn't seem to hear my argument that a great deal of scripture *is* presented as a history lesson. I mean, hello!? *Chronicles*? I even pointed out that I *always* end the session by looking at the scriptures people have used and *abused* in arguing their opinions about the events. The kids never seem to tell that part to their parents. And the adult chaperones in the room always leave to go to choir practice before we get to that part."

(At my farewell banquet a few years later, one very encouraging father told a behind-the-scenes story I had not heard. "My son came home complaining that Brad had led another history lesson that night. I asked what it was about. He told me. I had heard the name of one of the people he mentioned, but I didn't know much about him. I asked my son a question about him, but he didn't know the answer. So I pulled out an encyclopedia and we read the article. Then we started talking about how it could be helpful to know that, and what Brad was up to in presenting the information. I told him I wouldn't want him going to a church where the youth minister didn't challenge him to think." Then, the father turned to me. "Brad, thank you not only for challenging my son to think, thank you for challenging me, too.")

"So the youth *and* many of the parents are upset with me. But dad-blame-it, I just think it is the right thing to do. You and your generation did so much to make this world a safer and better place. Not perfect, but heroic. And I think we need to remember what happened and learn from it, both good and bad."

Virginia shook her head sadly. "Brad, I'm really grateful for what you are trying to do. I don't know what we're going to do with this generation. But I'm glad you're trying."

"Thank you, Virginia. But I didn't ask you to come in here to talk about youth Bible study."

Virginia did a double take.

"Let me ask you. And I want you to shoot straight with me." I paused. "Do you have any doubt of my patriotism or love of this country?"

"Heavens, no!" she said, offering a tone and look that was meant to condemn anyone who would suggest otherwise.

"Thank you. Now, in light of my question, why do you suppose I asked you to meet me in here?"

Virginia thought for a moment. Then she sighed, lowered her head, and, lifting only her eyes, looked toward the stage. There, respectively on either side of the pulpit, was an American flag and a Christian flag. Virginia began nodding her head.

The flags had materialized on the stage a few Sundays after our former pastor had retired. Our pastor served for 25 years, an extraordinarily long tenure for any minister to be at one church but particularly long for a Baptist. For that quarter of a century, a cold war of passive-aggressive combat had been waged over the placement of flags in the sanctuary. The pastor believed the sanctuary should be reserved for the worship of God, and flags in the sanctuary risked becoming civil idolatry. A group of World War II veterans saw the absence of the flag as a rejection of the country that provided the very freedom to worship in the first place. The flags would be brought out for vacation Bible school for the traditional pledges during opening assemblies. Then the pastor or the secretary would hide them. Eventually, one of the veterans, looking through a boiler room for a valve or something, would find the flags and put them back in the sanctuary. Then the shell game would begin anew.

During the pastor's long tenure, whenever the flags had materialized, they had been placed in the corners at the front of the sanctuary. Now that the pastor was gone, the veterans, to wave the banners of their liberation, had placed the flags immediately beside the pulpit.

Virginia raised her head full up, drew her shoulders back, and exhaled resolutely. "Brad, I just believe that if we are going to worship in freedom, we need to remember those who suffered and died so we can. My husband fought for that flag."

"Oh, Virginia! Don't sell what Raymond did so short." Virginia looked baffled, not offended. "Raymond didn't fight for that flag. He fought for the British flag, the French flag, the true German flag. He fought for every country and every person in the world needing to be freed from the tyranny of Hitler and Mussolini. In fact, in fighting against Hitler, he fought against a dictator who started his rule by *requiring* churches to display the Nazi flag."

"But that was the *Nazi* flag. Of course that has no place in worship."

"So the American flag stands for freedom, so it's OK?"

"Yes."

"You're opposed to abortion aren't you?"

"Yes."

"To the Pope, the American flag is a reminder of a country that has legalized abortion. And some have compared abortion to the Holocaust."

Virginia looked stunned by this argument. She turned her eyes to the side, looking for words, realizing that she couldn't say "but that's different." If she said in this argument that the Holocaust was different from abortion, then the next time she was arguing the issue of abortion, she would not be able to make that comparison. She looked at me, reluctantly conceding the point.

"See, I *love* the flag. I love singing the National Anthem. But when we come to worship, I want the focus to be on *God*. I don't mind having the flag for special occasions like the Fourth of July or vacation Bible school, because at times like that I always take the time to say we have it there to remind us of our need as Christians to be good citizens. You remember what I always say in vacation Bible school assembly?" She nodded, but I continued anyway. "Since we have lots of kids who are not U.S. citizens, I tell them, while we are pledging the flag, think about how you can be a good citizen for *your* country. It's not about being politically correct. It's about being *Christians* above all else and making sure we don't do anything that would cause someone to feel unnecessarily uncomfortable or unwelcome in *worship*. That being said, I will say that I have seen *one* church where I liked the way they had the U.S. flag displayed. I was channel surfing one time and saw a televised worship service. It caught my eye because behind the preacher there was a globe. Then around the wall they had every flag of the world. See, I think having every flag up says everyone is welcome here. When we gather in this room for worship, *every person* should feel welcome and focused on God. With the flags right there in the middle of the stage, it draws the attention to the flags rather than God. And practically speaking, my dad was visiting this past Sunday; he asked why the flags were on the stage blocking the view of the choir; he couldn't see the face of the soloist who was singing from the choir loft."

Virginia pursed her lips and sighed. She surveyed the front of the sanctuary. "What if we moved them over in the corners?"

"I think that would be discreet enough that visitors would know we are just acknowledging our citizenship responsibilities without making them feel excluded."

"OK," Virginia said, nodding. "Let's do that."

She held the flags reverently as I lifted the poles and bases and moved them to the corners of the sanctuary. We stepped back and examined our work. Virginia nodded her head in reluctant approval. I interpreted the reluctance as her anticipating assuaging the veterans who might see her as having caved. I realized this was an accurate interpretation when she said, "I'll tell the boys."

"Thanks," I said. "That's what I appreciate about you... and what I appreciated about Raymond. We don't always agree, but we shoot straight with each other and work it out." Virginia nodded and smiled.

I looked at the flags and remembered reading about the Nazi flag being draped on German pulpits and communion tables. "By the way. Have I told you when I first knew something was special about those who stood up to the Nazis?" Virginia shook her head.

"When I was about 6 or 7 years old, we drove down here to Knoxville to see *The Sound of Music*. You remember the scene where Captain Von Trapp gets home from his honeymoon and tears down the

Nazi flag that had been placed on his house?" Virginia nodded and smiled. "When he tore the flag in half, my dad stood up and applauded. I remember being startled and then self-conscious, because Dad was the only one applauding. I didn't understand it at the time, but as I got older and learned more history, every time I've seen that movie I remember my dad clapping at that scene. Flags are powerful symbols. We have to be careful how we display them. I appreciate Raymond helping tear down the Nazi flag. I appreciate you helping display ours… less obtrusively."

Virginia smiled and nodded.

Sometimes our harbors, our sanctuaries— places intended for safety— become the objects of conflict. Sometimes in our church sanctuaries we fight over the color of the drapes, and sometimes we fight over where to drape our nation's colors. Sometimes, as with the sailors on the U.S.S. West Virginia, we are wounded because of mistakes beyond our control. Sometimes, as with the sailors on the U.S.S. Tennessee, those same mistakes are what caused us to be spared. And often the things that protect us, be they surrounding ships or traditions, become the barriers to our progress. When that happens, sometimes the best we can do is take the time to clear a path and then limp back home for repairs.

**Questions for Reflection**
1) One of the suggested steps in peacemaking is to find some point of common ground. How did that happen in the described scenarios?
2) Consider a conflict in your life. What possible common ground do you have with your opponent?

# CHAPTER 11

## Touching Stories

THE SCREAMS AND MOANS OF AN ELDERLY MALE and the rattling of bed rails filled the Coronary Care Unit. At the desk in the center of the unit, the charge nurse recorded notes in a chart, her gaze portraying the intent distraction of someone defusing a ticking bomb.

"Anything I can do, Mary?"

With uncharacteristic disgust, Mary said, "Get Bed Four quiet."

*Get Bed Four quiet.* There are several practical reasons for referring to patients by their bed numbers rather than their names. It protects their confidentiality if a visitor is present; it assures that Mr. Jim Smith does not get Mr. Mike Smith's sponge bath; and it speeds delivery of service when hospital personnel do not have to recall Mr. Mike Smith's location. But it never sounds as caring as the pragmatic motives intend. And on a unit with only eight beds, it sounds particularly callous.

Even with the sliding glass door closed, the sounds from Bed Four filled the Unit. Peering inside I saw a man I had seen before—figuratively speaking. Disheveled snowy hair. A chin straining up to yell revealed loose skin around an unshaven, pronounced Adam's apple. Eyes of gasping agony mixed with a paradox of anger, hurt, and resignation. Raising his knees to use his heels to press upward, his hospital gown slid down his bony thighs that framed his genitals and skinny buttocks. He had padded cuffs around his wrists and white cords around the cuffs restrained the backs of his hands to the bed.

When I arrived beside him, he looked into my eyes with a gaze similar to one I had seen before. But Bed Four's gaze was more . . . innocent, less hostile, but still agonized. I saw his name written on the white board over his bed. "Hello, Mr. Oliver. I'm Brad. I'm one of the hospital chaplains." He stopped screaming, but from the look in his eyes I might as well have spoken Cantonese and said I was a Sherpa come to assist his ascent up Mt. Everest.

Unlike the first time I had met this situation, this time, I didn't hesitate. I laid my hands on his shoulders just beside his neck. I just let them lie there for a moment. He batted his eyes closed. Slowly, and ever so gently, I began kneading his trapezius muscles, the muscles over the collar bones curving down from the neck. His mouth fell open. In less than five minutes he was softly snoring.

I covered him with a sheet and walked back to the nurses' station to enter my notes in his chart and read his case history. The chart was so thick it was almost time to start a second volume. As I suspected, based on my previous experience, Mr. Oliver had a long history of being institutionalized. In fact, he had the longest possible history. He had been a foundling, raised in an overcrowded, understaffed orphanage. He was in his eighth decade of life and had never lived outside an orphanage or asylum. Sitting at a desk a few feet from the charge nurse, I began writing my notes in the chart. Out of the corner of my eye I saw the nurse abruptly stop and look up like an Irish setter flushing a covey of quail.

"What happened?" Mary asked.

"What do you mean?" I asked.

"It's quiet. What did you do to Mr. Oliver?"

What did I do *to* Mr. Oliver; not what did I do *with* Mr. Oliver. Had I injected him with a sedative? Held a pillow over his face until he passed out? Hit him over the head with an oxygen tank?

"I rubbed his shoulders."

"You did what!?"

"I rubbed his shoulders. Have you read the man's chart? He's been institutionalized all his life. He's rarely, if ever, been touched except to be given a shot or tied down. Next time he's thrashing around like that, have somebody rub his shoulders, maybe even his feet."

In case review, I presented the incident with Mr. Oliver. One of my older colleagues was surprised the hospital did not have a massage therapist. Out of the case review, I decided to do a clinical paper on the importance of appropriate touch. One of my fellow chaplains recommended I read *Touching: The Human Significance of Skin* by Ashley Montagu. A few years earlier, when I encountered the man of whom Mr. Oliver reminded me, I had suspected the existence of a condition; in reading Montagu's book I discovered the terminology for that condition: touch deprivation.

When I was in seminary, I had worked PRN (i.e., as needed) as an aide at a hospital-based psychiatric clinic in Louisville, Kentucky. One afternoon, I was called in to work on the adult psych unit. It had been several weeks since I had worked that unit, having spent most of my recent shifts on the adolescent unit. I unlocked the unit and walked to the nurses' station for shift briefing. The TV monitor of the seclusion room caught my attention. An elderly man was in five point restraints on the bed— leather straps secured his wrists and ankles to the frame of the bed, and another broad strap wrapped around his waist. That was not too unusual. What was unusual was seeing The Big Guns all gathered in the room. Two widely published psychiatrists, their interns and another suited man I had never seen before, were standing shoulder to shoulder.

"What's going on in there?" I asked the nurse, gesturing at the monitor.

"Oh, that is so sad. They're in there with Mr. Legion."

"Mr. Legion?"

"You don't know Mr. Legion?"

"I haven't been on this unit in a *long* time."

"I guess not. He's been here for nearly five months or so. The last two or so he hasn't even been able to go home on weekends. He just keeps getting worse. He's completely psychotic now. And the man's filthy rich. The irony is, he's given a lot of money over the years to mental health causes."

The first time I made rounds, I walked past the seclusion room just as the Fab Five were walking out. There was not a trace of the pompous air I usually sensed in those I had met before. They looked . . . genuinely concerned . . . even humble.

A few nights later I was called in to work the night shift. The nurse told me it was going to be a long night. We were understaffed for a relatively high census. To make matters worse, Mr. Legion required one-to-one care. He was manic, was walking feverishly, but kept falling, so needed someone to walk with him round the clock. I was to be his crutch.

When I walked down the hall toward his room, the aide I was relieving looked up from the rocking chair where he was thumbing through a magazine outside Mr. Legion's room. He looked at me with relief and smug pity.

"He's resting right now, but that won't last lon... ."

Mr. Legion bolted up from the bed. "Come on, let's go!" he barked.

My predecessor said, "Good luck," patted me on the back and hastened away down the carpeted hall.

I stepped into the room to steady Mr. Legion as he began to stand. His voice was strong but slightly slurred, his movements were quick and robotic, but his eyes were strangely both empty and electric. With jerking steps he hustled out of his room. He was leaning forward precariously. His arms were covered with bruises, and his left cheekbone blackened. I eased my right hand around his left elbow and my left hand into his left hand. He tried to snatch it away and nearly tumbled down. I steadied him. Three steps later he tugged less forcefully. Two steps after that he yanked my hand toward his face, lurched forward, and tried to bite me. I stopped the progression of my hand toward his mouth while saying the extremely reflexive and terribly therapeutic word "UHNT!" Wild-eyed, Mr. Legion spat at me, while trying to yank away. "LET GOAH ME GODDAMMIT!" But immediately he began walking again, seemingly torn between not wanting to need help, but knowing he wouldn't get far without it.

We shuffle-raced up the halls of the L-shaped unit twice, passing the nurses' station and patient lounge area at the intersection of the halls. The second time we passed his door, he led me into his room where he literally dived into his bed, a solid state bed, permanently connected to the floor with a wooden base and much lower than the typical hospital bed. I walked to the door and sat down in the rocking chair in the hallway. Also unlike typical hospital rooms, the lavatories in these rooms were in the back. So, sitting in the doorway, I was just a few feet from the foot of the bed. I sighed, collected myself, and was just starting to rock when… .

"Let's go!" he said. And we returned to our walking.

This cycle went on for two hours. Sometimes the rest stops were longer than others but never more than 10 minutes, usually less than five, and often just a few seconds. When Mr. Legion dived face down into his bed at 1:00 a.m., I was exhausted.

"God," I prayed. "I can't do this much more. What do I do?" At that moment the phrase "Jesus touched" caressed my mind. In the preceding months, while reading my Bible I had been giving attention to the verbs associated with the stories of Jesus. Red-letter editions of the Bible, highlighting things Jesus said, are common place. I had heard that some publisher had developed a green letter edition of the Bible, highlighting the actions of Jesus. Inspired by that, I was giving special attention to the actions of Jesus. I was struck by the number of stories with rich images of tactile actions taken by Jesus. Touching a leper; sticking his fingers in a deaf man's ears; rubbing mud into a blind man's eyes, spitting on and replacing an amputated ear.

Jesus touched. I laid my hands on the back of Mr. Legion's shoulders. He raised up. I gently resisted and pressed him back down. I started kneading his trapezius muscles. He exhaled a sigh. He was stiff, but his face, turned to the side, revealed eyes that seemed relieved. I quickened and slightly deepened my massage. Mr. Legion collapsed into his pillow; his eyes partially closed, appearing soothed. In less than five minutes he was softly snoring.

I plopped down in the rocking chair. This time I got to sit down for just over half an hour. When he woke up this time, Mr. Legion did not say, "Let's go." Instead, he raised his head, still face down, craned around toward me and with still electrified eyes matter-of-factly asked, "Will you rub my back again?"

"Sure," I said. I walked over beside him and began kneading his shoulders again. This time, however, I moved down to the shoulder blades, then middle back. Then I moved to his thighs just above his knees, then calves. His feet were callous and scaly. I touched them anyway. Mr. Legion sighed. I rubbed some more. He moaned his approval. I knelt at the foot of his bed and rubbed his feet until he began snoring again. This time he slept until 4:00 a.m. When he awakened abruptly he immediately said, "Will you rub my feet again?"

"Sure," I said. I returned to kneel at the foot of his bed and once again rubbed my hands on his mangled feet, gently pressing my thumbs into the arches.

Out of the corner of my eye, a female, middle-aged, African-American aide appeared in the doorway, clipboard in hand, making rounds to assure everyone was where they were supposed to be. A few seconds later I heard her whisper, apparently to one of the nurses, "Dat boy in dair is rubbin' dat crazy old man's feet. I wouldn't *touch* dat old so-and-so." Soon Mr. Legion was snoring again.

He was still sleeping at 7:00 a.m. when I left. The next day my phone rang just before midnight. An aide had called in sick at the last minute. Would I come sit with Mr. Legion again?

Just after I arrived, Mr. Legion woke up. He looked at me, and I saw the recognition in his eyes. "Will you rub my feet again?"

"Sure," I said. Once again, I rubbed his feet until he fell asleep.

Around 4:00 a.m. he woke up and said he was hungry. I got him a bowl of cereal and some juice. He sat at his table in his house coat and slippers, hair combed, looking like a wise old uncle. When he finished eating he looked at me with an alert gaze. The manic, frenzied look was gone. He looked coherent. With a clear voice he asked, "Where did you learn to make people feel so good?"

I grinned and shrugged. "I just like to make people feel like I like to feel."

"You a student?"

"Yes."

"U of L?" he asked, referring to the University of Louisville.

"No. Over at the Baptist seminary."

Mr. Legion recoiled in disgust like I had just had him unwittingly stick his finger in a stool sample. The corner of his mouth twisted into disdain, and there was particular venom in the last word of his next question. "You gonna be a *preacher*?"

I still didn't know what I wanted to be when I grew up. I shrugged my shoulders while indecisively nodding my head from side to side rather than back and forth and said, "That's a possibility."

A look came into Mr. Legion's eyes. It was a look of conviction in a man utterly in touch with his thoughts and in control of his feelings. It was the look a successful stockbroker would give a client who was thinking of investing a fortune in a bankrupt company. He leaned forward. His gaze imprinted itself on my skull at the rear of my brain. "Let me tell you something," he said with the voice of a mentor. "You can do more good doing this than you can preaching."

I raised my eyebrows and nodded to acknowledge receipt of his advice. I knew better than to speak. This was no time to be defensive about the vitality of preaching. This was no time to explore what negative experience may have contributed to his aversion to preachers. This was the time to absorb the passion of one who was preaching *to me* in the tradition of the apostle who said "faith without works is dead," that without love words are empty; this was the time to absorb the words of Jesus saying to me through Mr. Legion, "Whatever you do to the least of these . . . you do to me."

I wasn't called back to that unit for just over two weeks. As soon as I arrived, I checked the census sheet.

"Where's Mr. Legion?" I asked the charge nurse.

She dropped her pen and looked up, mouth open, shaking her head in amazement. "That is the wildest thing. Two weeks ago or so" (she shrugged) "he just got better. And we had to let him go. It was amazing. I don't know what happened."

I don't know either. When I was working on my clinical paper, I wrote a letter to Mr. Legion's psychiatrist asking permission to interview Mr. Legion. The doctor sent my request to Mr. Legion, but I never heard from him.

I do know what happened to the next critically ill patients I touched. They died.

Mrs. Talitha lived in a suburban condominium. I had never seen her at church in the time I had been there, and I certainly did not remember meeting her daughters who called me requesting a visit. I thought when they opened the door I might recognize a face I had seen in the congregation at Christmas or Easter, but I didn't.

The thirty-something daughter who greeted me at the door ushered me toward the den area. One of her sisters, appearing in her forties, was in the kitchen trying to fan the last of her cigarette smoke into the stove's vent. She smiled and waved impishly. The other forty-something sister smiled and waved from behind a magazine. In hushed tones,
The Usher explained, "The Hospice nurse says Mother probably will only make it another week." She slowed her strides to delay our arrival at her Mother's bedroom. "What worries us, though, is that she's stopped talking. We know she *can* talk, she just *won't*."

Entering the dim room, the daughter said, "Mother. You remember Brad? He's one of the ministers down at the church." She looked at me, searching for recognition that was not possible. I was surprised at how healthy this dying woman appeared. She was not gaunt.

Her eyes were sad but still had a spark of vitality. I shook her hand. Her grip was neither limp nor strong.

"Here, Brad," the daughter said, sliding a chair to the head of her mother's twin bed on the right side, the left side being against the wall. "I'll leave you two alone."

I wish I could remember what I said. I don't. I do remember that eventually I held her right hand in one of my hands and stroked the back of it with the other. I asked her if she had a favorite hymn. "Anything," she said.

"How about *Amazing Grace*?"

She nodded.

Feeling somewhat self-conscious about being overheard by the daughters in the other room, I began softly singing. When I was done, Mrs. Talitha smiled and softly but quite audibly said, "Thank you, that was beautiful."

"You're welcome. Would you like me to pray with you before I go?"

She nodded.

I prayed. When I said "amen" and looked up, she had tears in her eyes. But she smiled and said, "Thank you so much."

I nodded. Then, while shaking her hand with my right hand, I laid my left hand on her forehead and said, "Bless you." She batted her eyes in thanks.

The Usher was on the phone when I emerged into the den. She stopped long enough to say thank you. One of the other sisters then showed me to the door.

The next day on the phone, The Usher's voice sounded elated and amazed. "Brad? This is Mellisa . . . Eugena Talitha's daughter. . . . I don't know what you did, but it worked. Mother liked to talked our ears off yesterday afternoon. She had not spoken in nearly three days. Now she's talking, *and* she looks *happy*. What did you do?"

I told her.

While I had not known Mrs. Talitha or her daughters, the next time I was at a person's deathbed, I knew the daughters quite well. One was my wife, Connie; the others were her sisters.

Several hours after my father-in-law died, my wife tearfully took my hands and said, "Thank you for having us touch Dad. If you hadn't been there we would all have just stood there not knowing what to do."

The phone call had come early in the morning as we were leaving for work almost three months to the day after Bill had been told he had three to five months to live. His esophageal cancer had returned, five years after surgery, and treatment was no longer possible. (We did not find out until after the funeral that the doctor had told Bill and Marsha that surgery would give him about five years.) The day he had returned from Vanderbilt having been told to go home and try to be comfortable, we brought the video camera and asked him to read Uncle Remus to our children. Our son being about to turn one year old would not remember his maternal grandfather. Bill had made it two pages before giving up giving the characters his trademark voices. One page later he apologized to the infant in his arms and said, "Pappa needs to rest." My wife hustled our son and daughter out of the room. Bill looked at me wide-eyed, trying to catch his breath. "I hope it's not going to be like this the whole time," he said.

When the call came, our daughter was already at school. We strapped our son into his car seat, and less than 30 minutes later, after driving across Knoxville and winding into Strawberry Plains, we were standing at Bill's bedside. If he were not in his own room, I would not have recognized him.

He was not conscious. Marsha had called when she could not awaken him. Two of Connie's four sisters also were in the room. Bill had the death rattle I had seen and heard so many times before. His mouth was agape, and after long pauses he lurched for air.

I knelt beside him and took his hand in mine. "I love you Pappa."

"Yes, we should touch him," Connie tearfully said to her sisters. I stepped out of the way. Connie stroked his head. One of her sisters now took Bill's hand. Another lightly rubbed his knee. They each said goodbye. After a number of minutes, the pause between breaths persisted. The girls stepped back. Marsha stroked his head. "Is he gone?" I put the fore and middle fingers of my left hand on his throat. "His heart beat is strong," I said, omitting that it was very irregular.

His skin was soft. Even his razor stubble was not prickly. In the den, one of my brothers-in-law was staring out the sliding glass door counting the doves eating birdseed on the patio. Bill had always bought birdseed in 100 pound lots. In the last few weeks Marsha had taken over slinging several cups of seed across the patio, and she had done so the night before. Bill was 69 years old when I felt his final heartbeat nearly five minutes after he stopped breathing. And at that moment—based on reconstructing the events later—the 69 doves my brother-in-law had counted suddenly and inexplicably flew away.

Coincidence? (A hawk happened to fly by?) Metaphysical? (The birds sensed something?) Physical? (When Connie's sister picked up the phone to call hospice, some sound was made that startled the doves?) I don't know why the largest number of doves ever counted on Bill's patio happened to match his age and seemed to depart with his spirit. But I know that whatever the cause, it felt good.

It felt good when a much different Billy said, "I wished I'd known you when you got married. I would have gotten you something." Nothing he could have given me would have meant more than that comment.

During seminary, Connie and I served two summers as co-youth ministers at a church. When we arrived the first summer, there was quite a controversy swirling around the fact that the laundry mat across the street from the church had changed hands and the new owner had converted it into a pool hall. It wasn't just any billiard parlor; it was the rough kind: sharks, hustlers, pushers. Having heard Tony Campolo's story of throwing a birthday party for a prostitute, I decided to start hanging out at the pool hall.

Once a day I'd go over and just start playing. Billy approached me early on and asked if I wanted to play for $5. "Nah. I don't like to bet; I just play for fun." He'd have to try to hustle someone else. When he'd get bored he'd come play me for fun. I once overheard him say to someone, "Nah, he's a Christian, he don't bet; he just plays for fun." One day he was standing at a 90 degree angle from the top of the triangle of balls I was about to break. I hit the cue ball as hard as I could. The ball hit the one ball and shot into the air straight at Billy's head. He was propped on his cue, but caught the ball an inch from his head without blinking and then nonchalantly handed me the cue ball. To this day I wonder what he was on. Marijuana and alcohol tend to dull reflexes. But his dilated eyes and catlike reflexes were juiced by something.

Just before the end of the summer and our return to seminary, I learned that Billy was getting married. I was pretty much broke. But I went to a local salvage store and bought a brand new set of 6 juice glasses. I wrapped them and presented them to Billy. He teared up, looking like Agnes "holding her birthday cake like it was the Holy Grail" in Campolo's story. "Wow," he said. "I wish I'd have known you when you got married; I would have gotten you something." What a gift.

When Connie and I got out of seminary, a church member gave us a great deal on a house that had a pool table. One winter night I was driving home from church and saw a young man walking beside the road; he was wearing only a pair of pants and a tank top shirt. I recognized him as a teenaged boy who had visited our church a few times a year or two before. I hadn't seen him in a long time. I pulled alongside him, rolling down my window. "Joe-Joe?"

"Hey."

"Where's your COAT!?"

He gave an embarrassed grin, shaking his head. "I lost it in a poker game."

"You doofus. Get in here; I'll give you a ride." He got in. "I haven't seen you in a coon's age. Where you been?" I wasn't prepared for the answer.

"Juvie."

"What?"

"Juvenile detention. You know— kid jail."

"What? How long were you in?"

"A year."

"A year!? Joe-Joe, I had no idea! I'd have come to see you."

"It's alright. I got to play a lot of pool. That was our reward if we followed the rules."

"You any good?"

"Ok, I guess."

"Bet I can beat you."

He snickered.

A few minutes later we were in my basement. I didn't have to let him win. He smoked me. And I can hold my own.

When he sunk his last shot, I stepped over to the basement closet and opened the door, revealing my variety of coats. "OK. You beat me. Pick one."

"No. I'm not taking one of your coats."

"Joe-Joe. You think I want it getting around town that I Welshed on a bet? You're not leaving here without a coat."

He stepped over to the door. I held my breath; would he pick my favorite coat? He reached and got the blue down coat with the red flannel lining covered with ducks. It was the coat I was wearing the night in college that Connie and I took a long walk in the park. I had a picture of us, but it was the smell of that coat that reminded me of that night. It looked really good on Joe-Joe. I drove him home. My headlights illuminated an overgrown yard full of junk. As he got out I said, "Joe-Joe. No more poker for your coat, OK?" He laughed. "All right." I don't know if he kept his word or not. But he was warm that night.

I don't know why Mr. Legion got well. I'd like to think my actions had something to do with it. I don't know what ever happened to him or Mr. Oliver or Billy or Joe-Joe. I do know that Mrs. Talitha improved after I held her hand and sang to her. I don't know if our touching Bill did anything for him, but I know it did a lot for us. Touching may not always cure, but, done appropriately— whether with a direct touch or via a cheap set of juice glasses or a beloved down coat— it can still be healing, even if all that is healed is the fear of death and the feeling of isolation. I will leave to others to quantify the significance of touch. What I do know is this: if I am hurting, I hope someone will rub my feet; if I am dying, I hope someone will hold my hand, stroke my head, and sing with me.

**Questions for Reflection:**
1) What differentiates appropriate and inappropriate touch?
2) In most of these situations I was alone with the patients. Consider the possible pitfalls of this. How could these pitfalls be avoided?
3) What are other pitfalls of touching and how can they be addressed or avoided?
4) If a patient is coherent, how do you gain permission to touch them?*
5) How may religious rituals, such as prayer and anointing, lend themselves to being an entrée to touching?

*A reviewer rightly took issue with me using the singular noun "patient" with the plural pronoun "them." I for one think it is high time the English language had a gender neutral pronoun. Since rules are determined by usage, I am hereby contributing to formalizing the usage. (But until the American Psychological Association changes the rule in their style manual, I will continue to deduct points on my students' papers.

# CHAPTER 12

## Congruence

"What are you mad about?"[2]

"I'm not mad about anything," I said flatly, caught somewhat off guard by the suddenness of the question. My Clinical Pastoral Education (C.P.E.) supervisor, leaning back in his swiveling desk chair throne, cocked an eye at me with a patronizing smirk that said *you are in such denial*. With a tone of a dog trainer dealing with a cute but slow-learning beagle, he asked again, "What are you mad about, Brad."

"I'm not mad about *anything*!" I said, my voice in a squeaky *falsetto*.

"What are you mad about, Brad?"

"Well *now* I'm mad that you're hounding me about what I'm mad about when I'm not mad about anything!"

"THERE!" my supervisor blurted out, pointing at my foot.

"What?"

"What did you just do with your foot?"

I looked at my right foot, planted firmly by the right front leg of my chair. I looked back at my supervisor with a gaze that said, *are you high?*

Hannibal pursed his lips. He was about to have me for dinner, but I was three-day-old leftovers instead of the fresh lamb chop he was craving. I stared at him in silence.

---

[2] This is a reprise of an anecdote from Chapter 4, included here for those not reading consecutively.

He slapped his foot on the floor. "Are you aware that every time you've ended a sentence, you've been slapping your foot on the floor?" he asked rhetorically.

I wrinkled up my nose and one corner of my lips.

"You've been punctuating your sentences with a tap of your foot," he said, punctuating his statement with a firm tap of his foot on the floor. "That" (he repeated the tap) "is a gesture of anger." He tilted his head and looked at me with a compassionate sigh. "Look, I know we're taught that anger is a bad thing. And I suspect you're so conditioned to deny your anger that you really believe you're not angry. But our bodies usually communicate what we're really feeling, and your body language is saying you're mad." He paused. "Part of my job is to help you become aware of your feelings. You can't be congruent with your feelings if you don't know what they are."

Congruent. There was that word. I had been hearing it since counseling class in college when we studied Virginia Satir. Satir maintained that congruent people could identify their true emotions and communicate them in a productive manner rather than disguising them by blaming others, using humor as a mere distraction, acting intellectually superior, or avoiding any conflict.

My supervisor was always pressing me to identify my *feelings*. "No, I didn't ask you what you are *thinking*; I asked you what you are *feeling*." He would wait, then give me the four options. "Mad, glad, sad, or scared." Every emotion was a variation of one of these.

One day in our weekly supervision meeting, I was stunned by his reaction to my candor. He wanted me to be congruent; I'd give him congruent.

"Where do you want to start?" he had asked.

"I want to start with the fact that I'm upset with you."

He raised his eyebrows with the successful smirk of Professor Higgins, gratified that Eliza Doolittle had, with a mouth full of marbles, properly annunciated, "The rain in Spain stays mainly in the plain."

"Yesterday, I was sitting there in the outer office working on some paperwork. You were in here talking to that guy who used to be one of your interns."

"John," my supervisor informed me. (His eyes twinkled with delight. I knew that he knew where I was going, and he was going to tear me to pieces for being too sensitive or something.)

"You all were talking about other employees here at the hospital. John started talking about [one of the hospital administrators]. You said, 'He puts on a good front, but he's basically a very shallow person.'" My supervisor nodded, agreeing with the accuracy of my recollection of the conversation. "I thought it was very inappropriate for you to be disparaging another hospital employee, especially in open earshot of an intern." My supervisor continued nodding pensively. To my confusion, though, he looked like he was admiring me— and not like a delicious morsel he was about to devour but like a fellow pilgrim. I had just reported a thought; he would wonder how I *felt*. "And I was upset that you put me in such an awkward position and disappointed that you would do something so unprofessional."

"You're right," he said with sincere penitence in his voice. "It was inappropriate. I apologize."

We stared at each other. I could see the genuine remorse in the eyes of The Individual, but beneath I could see The Supervisor thinking *see, that wasn't so bad was it?*

"Thank you," I said.

He bounced his head forward once and batted his eyes to say "you're welcome."

I had done it! I had been congruent with my thoughts and feelings! My C.P.E. supervision was painful, but it was ministry boot camp, and my Drill Sergeant had to ride me hard to prepare me for combat on the front lines. Now I was armed with congruence.

It worked well at boot camp. It took me several years to figure out that the youth in my church did not want a congruent drill sergeant for a youth minister. I had been an employee and student of my supervisor; my youth did not *have* to come to church and they had not signed on for an intensive in-your-face confrontation to unseat their denials.

I thought that if I modeled congruence, it would help instill congruence. The day I confronted my supervisor, it was as if he had yelled, "He's alive!" But then I broke out of the hospital into a local parish to terrorize the villagers.

It started at my very first event at my new church. It was a social in the home of a church member after Sunday evening worship. A dozen or so youth, mainly middle schoolers, were gathered in a circle around the den, eating chips and sipping soda. "Let's play Psychiatrist!" someone said. "Yeah!" several voices rang out.

"I'm not familiar with that game," I said. It was then explained that in the game Psychiatrist, someone is sent out of the room; the group then picks a famous person to describe; the person is brought back in the room; proceeding around the room, each person offers a description of the celebrity, and the person who was sent out tries to guess who it is.

A few rounds into the game, an eighth grade boy name Tyler was sent out of the room while the group decided on someone for him to identify. Wanting to add a new twist to the game I said sneakily, "Hey, what if the person he's trying to identify is himself?" The room ignited with delight. Someone fetched Tyler. He returned with the sheepish grin of a teenaged boy being watched by the world.

The first person in the circle said, "I'm a male."

"Are you... Brad Pitt?" Tyler inquired. A smattering of snickers ricocheted around the circle.

"No," the first person said, turning to the second.

"I'm a musician," came the second description.

"Hmm. Male musician. Are you Garth Brooks?"

"Nope."

The third person in the circle was a boy named Justin, who happened to be a good friend of Tyler, though very different. Justin was handsome and athletic. Tyler was athletic but was more of a bookish, band geek. Justin grinned slyly. "I'm a sissy."

The room exploded in laughter. My wife and I exchanged pained and angry looks across the room. I felt responsible for not anticipating this type of turn of events.

Tyler combined the information he had so far. "Are you Michael Jackson?"

All the kids laughed. Tyler looked puzzled with what was so funny about the guess. In retrospect I wish I had called timeout, sent Tyler out of the room, and told the group we had to find someone else who met the descriptions so far. But I was paralyzed by my shock.

Tyler kept asking questions. Suddenly he said, "Oh! Me!"

The room once again exploded with the laughter of everyone but my wife and me. I watched as Tyler returned to his seat, smiling but blushing. I watched his eyes as he rewound to Justin describing *him* as a sissy.

The next Wednesday at church I called Justin into my office. Instead of starting with the question, "How do you think Tyler felt when you described him as a sissy?" I started with an effort at congruence. "I was upset with what happened Sunday night at the social when you described Tyler as a sissy. I know sometimes we get caught up in a game, but I thought that was very insensitive and even cruel." A look of shock came into Justin's eyes. *Good*, I thought. He'll see that I can be angry but will still care about him. I smiled. "Tell you what, I want to do a lesson on the dangers of name calling, and I want you to help me. Why don't you go home, get on the Internet, find an article about the harmfulness of name-calling and let me know what you find?" Justin shrugged and said flatly, "OK."

    I went home very self-satisfied. Just as my C.P.E. supervisor had assigned me to sit alone in a waiting room, and the experience had been a revolutionary epiphany for me, I was giving Justin an assignment that would make him a better human being, and maybe one day he would use the same wise method when he became a leader. I felt very successful. Then Justin's father called me. Justin had told him of our talk and my assignment, and his father was calling me to let me know he thought I was overreacting. He was very congruent, so congruent I didn't sleep all night. But somehow I managed to miss the lesson in that. Somehow I missed the fact that if I got so wounded by a harsh tone of voice that a teenager, far less equipped than I, might feel wounded rather than admire my congruence. Somehow I missed the fact that it is one thing to report a feeling; it is another to do it with a harsh tone and facial expression or the exercise of power such as making an assignment. Somehow I missed the fact that what works in a school setting with compulsory attendance may not work in church. Somehow I just kept trying to be a C.P.E. supervisor to my youth. Granted, sometimes it actually "worked," which is to say all's well that ends well. Justin, his father, and I went on to have a great relationship, as did Justin and Tyler.

    As I look back I see a number of similar encounters that worked out— even worked out well, but it was only because of blind luck or that, as one of my seminary professors used to say, "God can draw a straight line with a crooked stick."

I once got very frustrated with a mother who was extremely overprotective of her children; and I was almost more frustrated with the father who wouldn't seem to intervene. After our group safely returned from a trip, the father sighed and said to me, "I was hoping the kids making it home fine would show Jane the kids aren't going to die if they leave the house. She drives me crazy. We spend so much time fighting about her overprotection of the kids. For crying out loud, she wouldn't let Tim go to a basketball game with Sammy Brooks *and his parents* unless he took a cell phone and called home every hour."

I raised my eyebrows in disbelief.

"See what I have to deal with?"

"Have you considered going to see a counselor?"

"I've begged her."

Tears welled up in his eyes. "She's such a good person. She's just obsessed that something terrible is going to happen to the kids. She just can't shake nearly losing them when they were babies and that we can't have any more."

I wondered what else may have been contributing to her obsession. I never found out in her case, but I have always found that when someone's behavior seems out of kilter, some life experience is feeding it—some experience that makes it make sense and helps me feel more compassionate. Such was the case in dealing with another parent's reaction to his daughter attending a camping trip.

It had started raining about an hour before sunrise. It had been a great weekend: brisk October mountain air, blue skies, autumn leaves ablaze with color. Now we were breaking camp in the rain and riding home all wet and sticky.

When we arrived at the church, the sun was out. Gone was the brisk mountain air. The humidity made breathing a chore.

I had been stuck so many times cleaning the van myself that I made a rule that "the trip is not over until the van is cleaned and the gear is stowed; parents, please do not take your children until the jobs are done." This time there was *a lot* of cleaning to do. We had muddy tents and tarps that had to be hosed off and spread out to dry. All our cooking gear had to be washed. I assigned a set of parents to supervise the outdoor work while I took charge of the kitchen and supply closets where I knew the storage locations of particular items. I did *not* want to be on the bad side of the church hostess. (Once she had harshly fussed at me when her 5-gallon sugar container was found empty after a fund raiser car wash. "*Brad!* Do you know what happened to my sugar? I had at least another three cups of sugar in this." "What? That's a sugar container? I thought that was powdered dish washing detergent. We ran out of soap at the car wash, and I sent that outside to wash with." She screeched, "You what!? *You mean you don't know the difference between sugar and dish powder?*" With matching harshness I replied, "Oh, I know the difference when I'm not in a hurry and I take the time to taste it. But *I* don't normally store sugar in a five gallon container *next to the dish washer!*" I later apologized for my tone, only to be ridiculed as stupid in front of the kitchen staff.)

I was scrambling around trying to be everywhere at once. In retrospect I know why. When I was in high school, since our church was next to a busy highway, I proposed that our church erect a live nativity scene. It became a huge success and an annual event featuring live animals from a local petting zoo. But the first year we had many gremlins. The Saturday before Christmas we had a work day to build the nativity scene and set up the fellowship hall for a banquet. Our new pastor did not know which end of a hammer to pick up. He knew his limitations and opted to work where his strengths lay: while all the men were outside in a cold rain driving nails into planks, the pastor and the women were inside decorating. At one point my father came up to me; he was drenched and glaring mad. "When you become a pastor, if you tell a bunch of men to show up to work in the rain, you better be outside working with them, not working inside." Thus, I spent most of the early years of my ministry running here and there making appearances, trying to do everything. Maybe my father's expectations were unrealistic. Maybe my pastor could have done a little proactive public relations. Whatever the case, the upshot was that I was terrified of people being angry with me because I asked them to do something or of being somewhere doing something when people really expected me to be somewhere doing something else.

After the campout I had parents inside washing dishes and outside cleaning tents (probably wondering why I wasn't out in the heat with them). I was bouncing back and forth frantically trying to look busy at both fronts. As I hastily attempted to transfer a carton of eggs from a cooler to the refrigerator, the carton lid popped open and one of the eggs splattered on the floor. At the moment of impact a voice said, "Brad! Margaret Jones needs to see you outside. She said she's in a hurry." *Oh, no. What have I done or not done now?* "I'll be back to clean that up in just a minute," I informed the father and daughter working in the kitchen. I bound outside and was relieved to find Mrs. Jones smiling. "Hey, Brad. I know you're busy but I wanted to give you some news. My biopsy came back, and it was benign."

"Oh, Maggie, that's great!"

We talked about her news for a number of minutes. What was I supposed to do? *OK. Glad you're not going to die. Gotta go!* No. I needed to minister to her. I was trying to do just that when Mr. Staid, the father working in the kitchen stopped up to us and said, "Brad! That egg you dropped is *still* in there on the floor. *You* need to *get in there* and clean it up!"

"I will get to that….." I started to say, "but I need to have this conversation right now," but I didn't want to make Mrs. Jones feel any more responsible than she already would.

"Well, you need to get your priorities straight," Mr. Staid blurted and stomped, embarrassed daughter in tow, toward his car.

Mrs. Jones looked at me with eyes that said both "I'm sorry" and "*Well*, what's his deal?"

What was his deal indeed? I was tempted to vent my anger by telling her about his odd behavior over the weekend. He had showed up at our campsite on Friday morning (the trip had coincided with the kids being out of school). He had driven two hours to deliver a box of two dozen donuts. We were leaving the campground to go on a hike just as he arrived. He did not want to go with us. When we came back a few hours later he was reclined impatiently on the hood of his car. His behavior was far out of the ordinary for him. He was one of the most encouraging parents with whom I had ever worked. Few men send mail, but I got handwritten thank you cards and letters from him a few times a year. What was going on?

The next day at church, I told my pastor everything that had happened. He nodded knowingly. "Thursday after you left, he and Mary found out that she has a tumor on her brain. She insisted on going to work on Friday. On top of the tumor, Megan apparently has been showing some signs of anorexia."

"Oh." I nodded. We looked at each other and simultaneously said, "the donuts." "Well I knew *something* had to be going on. Bless their hearts. How awful. Is the tumor operable?"

"Probably. But they have to wait for some more tests."

Waiting and fear. It's a dangerous combination that often leads to outbursts of anger.

Fear usually is at the root of my rash actions. The greater the fear, the more rash has been my action. The most frightening events of my career thus far have pertained to the safety of young people in my charge. In one such event I feared for the very life of the young man involved.

I was leading a group of families on a hike in the Great Smoky Mountains National Park. Before leaving the parking lot at Clingman's Dome, I gave a thorough briefing on the importance of staying together. I told stories of people who went missing and were later found dead. Then we hiked over three miles on a fairly rugged trail to the scenic overlook at Andrew's Bald. After a picnic and romp in the grassy meadow overlooking Fontana Lake, we started heading back. Among the hikers in our group was a father and his fifth grade son, Allen. Another father, who had recently started visiting our church was with his third grade daughter. Along the trail, the two fathers had struck up an immediate friendship and got started talking about their jobs and hobbies. I was so gratified that the trip I had planned was helping nurture a new friendship.

I was concerned, however, about the friendship blossoming between their respective son and daughter. Allen had a reputation for pressing every limit. (A few years before I had seen a normally mild mannered Sunday school teacher carrying him down the hall by the shoulders. He had set him down outside another class and said, "You wait *right there* until your parents come out; then you tell them why you're there!") I could tell that the girl was gah-gah over the attentions she was receiving from an older boy. What might he put her up to?

I was carrying my own daughter in an infant carrier on my back, leading our line of about a dozen hikers. I had assigned a parent to take up the rear and told the kids to stay between myself and that parent. At one point on the way back to the van, I stopped to adjust the pack. Allen was carrying one of the walkie-talkies. "Hey, Brad," he asked. "Can we walk up to the curve and see if the radio will pick up that far?" I looked up; the curve was about a hundred yards ahead. Distracted by the pack, I said, "Sure. Just stay where I can see you."

A few moments later Allen called on the radio, "Can you hear me, Brad?"

"Ten-four," I called back playfully."

"OK. I'm going to… "

I didn't hear the rest of what Allen said. But as he and the girl wheeled around and headed around the curve I guessed that what he had said was something about going further ahead. "Allen! Stop!" I called into the walkie-talkie. No answer. I knew the walkie-talkies were so weak that they would not transmit past the granite ledge Allen and the girl had just passed.

Fifteen minutes later a couple hiking the other direction met me on the trail. They saw the look in my eyes.

"Are you looking for a boy and a girl?" the man asked.

"Yes," I said emphatically.

They're *way* ahead of you, he said. They said if we saw you to tell you they'd see you at the van. We told them they ought to wait. They said they would, but after we got down the trail a little, I looked back and they were on the move again. Are you all going to the parking lot at Clingman's Dome?"

"Yeah."

"I hope they take the fork to the right."

"Yeah. Me, too," I said, looking at the fathers who still seemed oblivious to the danger.

When we arrived at the parking lot, Allen and the girl were sitting on the hood of the van smiling.

Allen's father led him to one side and mildly reprimanded him. I was livid. Allen was two years from coming into the youth group. I had no intention of allowing Allen to think such behavior would be acceptable on any trip I was leading. Thinking back to my own middle school years, I recalled the most heinous physical pain I had ever heard described when a friend of mine read me a passage from a book about torture during the Vietnam War. After Allen's father left, I approached Allen. He was wearing a leather choker necklace. Locking my gaze in his, I slid my fingers under the necklace and pulled him toward me. I did not want to appear to disapprove of what his father had said, so even though I had overheard every word, I said: "I don't know what your father said to you, but when you get in the youth group, if you pull a stunt like that I will drive toothpicks under your toenails and break them off. Are we clear?" I could tell Allen was contemplating how painful toenail torture would be. He nodded.

A few minutes later I approached Allen again. "Allen, you know I wouldn't really drive toothpicks under your toenails, right?" He nodded. "I said that because I wanted you to know just how serious I am. Buddy you scared me. You... and Cindy... could have *died*. It happens up here all the time. When I make a rule it is for your safety. OK?" He nodded. "Now, I won't drive toothpicks under your toenails, but please don't *ever* do anything like that again." He nodded again, and I hugged him. We got along grandly after that, and he became a model group member.

The same was true of Sam. Sam did not grow up in a church-going family. He started visiting our church with one of our members when he was in middle school and attended regularly throughout high school.

One Sunday night prior to having no school on Monday, a group of boys from the youth group asked if they could just spend the night at our house after a movie viewing. My wife and I agreed. The next day, I was driving the boys home one by one. Just before getting to his house, the last boy said, "Brad, I hate to rat on somebody, but I'm really upset with Sam. This morning while you were still asleep, Sam snuck outside and was smoking. He was coming out of the bathroom, and I saw him sneaking back in the house. I smelled cigarettes on his breath. I told him I couldn't believe that after you let us stay at your house he was doin' stuff like that."

"Thanks for telling me. Don't worry; I won't tell him you told me."

The next time the group was over, I invited Sam to go with me to a room overlooking the back carport where all the other guys were playing basketball. "Is this where you come to spy on us?" Sam asked.

"No. But you see all those houses out through there," I asked gesturing at the subdivision lots surrounding us, without making eye contact.

"Yeah," Sam affirmed.

"It amazes me," I continued matter-of-factly, "what my neighbors tell me they see going on in my back yard." Out of the corner of my eye I saw Sam's eyes widen. "You see Tommy right there?"

"Yeah."

"I know he does some things I don't approve of. But because I want him to feel welcome here and at church, I overlook some of that. *But if I ever found out he was getting other kids in the group to participate with him, I'd kick his butt clear up to his ears.*" I paused then cocked an eyebrow and glanced over at Sam. He was grinning nervously. "We clear?" I asked.

"Oh, yeah," Sam said with an emphatic nod.

The night the church threw me a going away banquet, Sam, now a few years out of high school, showed up just as things were winding up. He raced up to me and threw his arms around me. "Dude, I just found out you were leaving. I've been in Mississippi at Mom's. I just got back and called Angela. She told me she had just left your going away party. I said, 'What!?' and jumped in the car and raced down here. Man I can't thank you enough for all you've done for me. I smiled and thought about his 15th birthday. We had a weekly youth support group meeting. The day after his birthday he shared with the group that he had gotten nothing for his birthday. His deadbeat father was broke. His affluent mother, having been accused of buying his love, *would* not buy him anything. After church I had taken him to Wal-Mart and took him on a $50 spending spree. I remembered holding his hand in the emergency room and praying with him as he screamed in pain after a motorcycle wreck nearly killed him. Threatening to kick his butt to his ears probably would not be recommended in most ministerial manuals or child psychology books, but combined with the love he knew I felt for him, it all came out in the wash.

Unfortunately, over the years I've encountered far too many youth whose parents were not abusive in ways that would lead to legal intervention but still abhorrently damaging to their children. I was stunned speechless when I was standing outside the church for the umpteenth time waiting for Randy's parents to come pick him up. They were always late. Off in the distance we heard the testosterone-pounding approach of a classic muscle car. "They sent my uncle to get me," Randy said. "I'd recognize that engine anywhere. It's a '68 Camaro." He paused. "My dad is so jealous that my uncle has one." He grinned— to cover his pain as it turned out. "My dad used to have one just like it. He says the two worst mistakes he made were selling that car and having me."

I wish I had said something profound. I wish I had maybe said something like "I'd be proud to have you for a son." I was so angry that someone would say something like that to a child that my instincts told me that if I said anything it might undermine any good relationship Randy had with his father. Before I could think of anything to say, the uncle barreled into the parking lot, Randy jumped in, and smiled brightly as he waved goodbye— proud to be escorted in such a chariot.

I did have the opportunity to tell Andy's stepfather exactly what I thought and how I felt about his treatment of Andy. The first time I met Andy, he was a mess. He was 15 years old but looked like a 20-year-old street thug— exactly the look he was going for, and I'm pretty sure he was under the influence of some narcotic. And that was at school, in one of the rural towns I served while in seminary. Some of the youth I was visiting for lunch introduced me to him. He started coming to our church and became quite active.

One night my phone rang at about 11:00. I had just come home from seeing the most graphically violent war movie I had ever seen. I knew I was going to have trouble sleeping. My wife, Connie, was out of town. I assumed she was making a late check-in call. But when I answered I heard sobs and Andy bawled, "Brad, I need you to get over here! Please! My mom is freaking out!"

I threw on some clothes and raced about two miles to his house, arriving just before the police. As I rounded the last corner, my headlights fell upon Andy and his mother standing in the middle of the street. She was in her bathrobe and was screaming up at him as his mammoth body backed up. He could have killed her with a single punch, but he was a gentle giant.

The police pulled up as I was getting out of my car. I quickly introduced myself as a minister who had been summoned. As the officers approached, Andy yelled, "She's throwing me out of the house because I want to date a black girl.'

"THAT'S RIGHT!" his mother screamed. "THAT AIN'T RIGHT, AND IT AIN'T HAPPENING IN MY HOUSE!!!"

One of the police officers suggested that Mrs. Rathburn go inside with him and describe the problem. Actually he eventually was going to explain why she couldn't throw her 15-year-old son out of the house and onto the street in the middle of the night.

While they went inside, Andy sat down on the front stoop and told the other officer and me what had happened. He had asked if a girl from school could come over for dinner. His mother had excitedly said yes. His stepfather had driven him to the girl's house. When she had walked from her house and Mr. Rathburn had seen the color of her skin, he had said, "No way. She is not getting in this car." He had driven Andy home and told Andy's mom, "Do you know what kind of girl he was trying to bring over here?" Andy put his face in his hands and sobbed. The officer looked at me with a raised-eye-brow grin that said "can-you-believe-this?" Andy looked up from his hands, his face twisted in agony. The image, the words that followed, and the tone of voice are burned onto my brain. "My mamma hates black people more than she loves me."

Regardless of any miraculous progress the officer inside was making, I didn't feel good leaving Andy there. I gestured for the officer standing there to withdraw a few feet away with me. I explained to him that my wife was out of town and I didn't feel it would be prudent for me to offer to take Andy home with me. But I would call a church deacon, and if it was OK with Andy's parents, I would take him to their house for the evening. The next day our youth group was going for a hike in the mountains. By the next afternoon maybe cooler heads could prevail. The officer went inside and negotiated that plan, and Andy and I crashed in a spare rooms of one of the kindest families I have ever known. But I didn't sleep. I kept seeing a bayonet slowly being forced into my chest by a soldier whom I knew I— like the character in the movie I had seen— would not be able to overpower.

The next day after the hike, I called Andy's mom. She quickly told me that she wanted me to set Andy down and show him in the Bible where it says that interracial marriage is WRONG.

I said, "Well, actually, that's going to be hard to do. There are passages that some people THINK condemn interracial marriage, but it's just not true. One passage says that Christians are not to be unequally yoked, but that is talking about Christians marrying non-Christians. The other passage is in the Old Testament, where Jews are told not to marry people of certain countries, but that is not because of their race but because they worshipped other gods— even committing human sacrifice. Jews were told not to marry them because of religious, not racial reasons. In fact, in Song of Solomon, one of Solomon's wives— a Shulamite— is described as 'dark and comely to behold' and some folks translate that 'black and beautiful.'" There was a pause after my impromptu exegesis. But Mrs. Rathburn rebutted with stunning argumentation: "Well, I don't care about that." I was flummoxed but kept trying until we eventually negotiated a tenuous peace treaty.

It turned out to be only a brief cease fire. Before I even got to say goodbye, Andy was shipped off to another state to live with his father. But that arrangement only lasted a few months and Andy was sent back to his mother's. He had not been back long when I was summoned to mediate another conflict.

Andy had been accused of stealing from his stepfather— a wizened man who was old enough to be Andy's grandfather and who had retired from the army, where he had been a desk jockey. Andy's maternal aunt introduced herself at the door. Andy's mom had left to go cool off. Andy and his stepfather were sitting in the living room, nostrils flared.

I waded into the mediation. Andy's aunt watched in silence.

Eventually Andy pled his case by sharing his credentials as a good kid. At some point along the way, he had made a profession of faith, and I had baptized him. A few days before his baptism we had been driving down the interstate together. A car had come up beside us on Andy's side. The car had slowed to go parallel. The darkened window on the driver's side of the other car started going down and a hand emerged. A cigarette was flipped out and then the car sped on. "Gosh, for a second there, I thought that guy was pointing a gun at us." Andy said, "I did, too. But you would have been fine. I'd take a bullet for you, Brad." Then I realized that Andy had, in fact, leaned forward, shielding me.

It was that kind of big-heartedness and character that Andy referred to when I made the case that he did not deserve his step-father's ire. Mr. Rathburn's eyes narrowed as he sat in his easy chair like the cock of the walk—even though the chair's enormous size made him look even more like a shriveled desiccated prune of a man. In response to Andy's defense, he spat his venomous assault: "If you're such a good kid, why does your father not want you?"

Andy sprang from his seat on the couch. Fortunately, since he usually wore his shirt un-tucked, I was able to catch his shirt tail and—miraculously—hold back the hulk while using his momentum to pull me up. I threw my arm around him. If he had wanted to, he could have passed through my hold like it was air. But he let me hold him back and merely unleash a primal roar at this stepfather—who grinned sadistically with a look that said *good kid, huh?* I gently but firmly pushed Andy toward the hall. "Go to your room and turn on your stereo, loud." He complied, stomping off down the hall.

I sat back down and locked eyes with the staff sergeant. I did not attempt to soften my contempt. I seethed and gathered my words.

"I thought I had seen it all. But that was the cruelest, most despicable thing I have ever seen someone do. That was DISGUSTING."

Mr. Rathburn's glare softened ever so subtly but our eyes stayed locked. Out of the corner of my eye I saw Andy's aunt smile at me in admiration. (Later, Andy told me, "My aunt told me what you said. Thank you.")

"I'm sorry, Brad, but we've just had it," Mr. Rathburn said. His mother and I work so hard, and he just keeps taking advantage of us." (He wasn't completely wrong. Andy was, after all, a teenager. He certainly was no angel. But he had far more goodness than most kids in his situation.) Our conversation continued until some alternatives had been established and a plan formed.

The next summer our group was at summer camp. On about the third night, we were gathered in a circle under the starlight, having church group devotions. Other groups seemed to do the exercise like a sprint and head for some play before lights out, but our group liked to care for each other. A few of the kids shared stories of their dread to go back home. One gal began all out whining about her parents' rules— really harsh rules like having to be home by 8:00 on a school night and 11:00 on weekends. Suddenly Andy released the same kind of primal roar he had directed at his stepfather. In shock we all looked over at Andy who had his head in his hands. There was enough light from nearby street lights on the college campus that we could see clearly enough. Andy looked up, tears streaming down his face. "I am so SICK of hearing you guys griping about your parents." He changed to a mock whiney tone: 'My mom and dad make me come home.' Oh, boo who. You think you all got tough lives. You don't know crap. Do you know why I get to go wherever I want to go and do whatever I want to do! BECAUSE MY PARENTS DON'T GIVE A CRAP ABOUT ME!!!" He was sobbing now and tears were beginning to stream down the faces of everyone in the circle— especially the gal who Andy had interrupted. "I would give anything to have parents who had rules for me— who cared whether I lived or died."

My heart hurt for Andy, but, shrouded by the darkness where no one could see, I was gently smiling. Andy was accomplishing more with the group with his outburst than all my sermons and Bible studies combined. And... his anger was genuine and appropriate.

Righteous indignation too often gets swept away in the tide of political "don't judge" correctness. But both Jesus and Paul made judgments; they just didn't *condemn*.

Was I being judgmental when a father told me he was going to go home and beat the hell out of his son? Well, you be the judge. As he stormed toward the church exit, I said, "Hank! Stop!...Hank! If you take one step out that door, I'm calling the police!" He stopped. I pointed to my office, and he complied.

I had passed an edict that his son could not go on an outing because he had threatened to beat up another youth member. I felt the need to send a message that I would not tolerate such behavior, so I had called him and his parents into a room as everyone else was preparing to leave for the swimming pool. The boy apologized for his threat. I told him I accepted his apology but he had to learn there were consequences for his behavior and the group had to see that I would promote safety, so he would not be allowed to go swimming. He said he understood. The parents agreed. I walked away feeling very self-satisfied. But moments later the father was in my face. He was hyperventilating and frothing at the mouth when he bellowed, "My wife just ran to the car sobbing. You can mess with me, but don't you dare mess with my son and wife! I'm capable of disciplining my own son! I'm going to take him home and beat the hell out of him."

In my office I apologized for any appearance of overstepping my bounds. "Hank, I know you are having a hard time with T.J. right now. I thought I was doing you a favor by being the bad guy so you wouldn't have to be." He nodded. We went through some scenarios of what might happen when they got home: TJ might slam doors; TJ might use profanity toward his mother. For each one Hank promised he would stay in his room and not strike his child. He promised to call me if things escalated beyond the point he felt in control.

Should I have let Hank leave the building? Some would argue, "He has his way of parenting; it's not my way, but who am I to judge?" If you think it was wrong for me to judge Hank, how is it that you are making THAT judgment?

The challenge is to make judgments without condemning. Jesus made judgments; from the woman at the well, to the woman caught in adultery, to Zachaeus's cheating people, Jesus made the judgment that they were wrong. He told them to stop. But he didn't condemn them. How do we listen to our judgments and utilize them in a positive rather than a destructive way?

The movie version of *All's Quiet on the Western Front* depicts a platoon of World War I era soldiers going through basic training and then moving into combat. When the platoon arrives at the front lines, their new commander acknowledges they have just arrived from very grueling, comprehensive training. "Now it is my task to help you forget everything you just learned." The troops look confused. The officer goes on to explain that often what is learned in boot camp is not helpful in the reality of combat. In the context of World War I, the officer's observation makes particular sense. Soldiers going through boot camp were being trained by old school cavalry officers who had not faced machine guns or gas attacks. The constancy of change contributes to lag between the experiences of teachers and practical application outside the classroom. I resist the temptation to refer to life outside the classroom as "the real world." The challenges in school are very real; the education afforded generally is quite applicable. But we make a mistake if we do not acknowledge and prepare for the fact that basic training can never fully prepare us for life on the front lines. In fact, many of the tools we gain in basic training may be counterproductive on the front lines. We must, then, strive to identify areas where what we have learned *or our application of what we have learned* is not consistent with the events and challenges we are facing.

  A few years into my service in a local congregation, I went to homecoming at my alma mater, a small Baptist liberal arts college. I met several of my old professors in the religion department. I had started college as a religion major (graduated as a psychology major), so I had several courses with the religion faculty. I told each of them that I felt they had done a wonderful job preparing me for seminary and ministry in terms of theology. "But there is one serious omission in the curriculum," I said to my mentors. I paused for effect, leaned in and whispered, "You need a course entitled *Putting Up With Crap in Baptist Churches*." (I'm sure, however, the phrase "Baptist Churches" in the preceding sentence could be replaced by any organization.)

  It took a few years, but what I finally learned was that I was much better putting up with people's individual and corporate idiosyncrasies when I made a more concerted effort to deal with my own. It's almost as if examining the log of neurosis in my own eyes has helped me tolerate the mote of neurosis in others. It was one of those lessons that was one thing to hear in class but another to live in the heat of combat. My first counseling practicum was led by a professor who had grown up on a rural farm. On the first day of class he told us we were going to learn by doing; each student would share our stories and be counseled by the group under his supervision. "Why should you deal with your own experiences?" he asked. "I grew up on a farm. I like to compare the problems we have in life to cow manure. When I was a kid we used to have to shovel cow piles into a wagon. What I noticed was that when cow piles got baked hard in the sun, they wouldn't stink. But when you shoveled them up, sometimes they would break open, and the inside?— whew! The inside stunk. When we do counseling, we stir up people's [cow piles]." He paused, puckered his bushy wise mustache, cocked his bushy wise eyebrow, and peered at us over the tops of his glasses. "Let me say one thing very emphatically. You have no right to stir up somebody else's [cow piles] unless you've had your own stirred up."

It's one thing to know you need to stir your own cow piles; it's another thing to do it. It's one thing to be aware of your emotions; it's another to be able to communicate it in a manner fit for public consumption. Be too honest with our self-disclosure, and we look like whiners. Be too concealing, and we are insincere and hypocritical. How do we find the balance? In my training, congruence was *what* I was challenged to accomplish. *How* to do that is a work in progress. If congruence is "harmony," the challenge of bringing congruence between education and application is the challenge of bringing congruence between *what* and *how.*

**Questions for Reflection**

1) The four main emotions are mad, glad, sad, and scared. All emotions are variations of these. To what degree are others aware of what emotions you are feeling inside?

2) What is the difference between being honest with feelings and being an emotional exhibitionist?

## CHAPTER 13

### Dealing with Cleavage

WHEN I GET TO THE END OF MY LIFE, I hope I can still say it was the worst day of my life. I'm afraid there probably will be worse, but in my first 40 years, the day my church's "great thong controversy" came to a head... or tail... was the worst so far.

The straw that broke the camel's back was when I walked into Sunday school one morning, and I was greeted by a pair of almost entirely bare buttocks. The young lady was seated in the floor, as was the custom for most young ladies attending classes in our carpeted "youth lounge." That room had couches around the perimeter. (Our pastor had been opposed to this arrangement but had not said anything at the time. When our youth group had outgrown the lounge, we had moved it into the large classroom. Now the girls tended to sit on the floor and the boys sat on the couches.) The young lady's bare posterior was bordered at the south by the "waistline" of a pair of very low rise jeans; the northern border was a thin red elastic panty that red VICTORIA'S SECRET VICTORIA'S SECRET VICTORIA'S SECRET.... The hillocks were bisected by another red line, far too thin for any writing. I found an excuse to get everyone standing and tried to rearrange seating. But the girl ended up sitting on the floor again. Throughout the class, the teenage boys enjoyed their aerial view from the couch. That did it. I was writing a letter to all the parents of the group members.

I asked my pastor to review the letter. "I not only like it," he said, "I want you to add my name and let me sign it." In the letter, I said something to the effect that some of the girls might be changing clothes between the time they left home and the time they came to church. (This was an attempt at diplomacy; I knew the parents knew how their children were dressed.) I described some of the things I had seen and why is was distracting at the least and, at worst, inconsistent with the atmosphere we were trying to develop. I said it would be one thing for "fringe" children to feel welcome regardless of their attire, but our members needed to set a higher standard.

The phone started ringing before the postal carriers were three houses past the homes receiving my... no... our letter. Amazingly, not one father was upset about the letter. But the mothers? A woman scorned is air conditioning compared to a momma who feels her daughter has been impugned and her own maternal skills questioned.

Before I continue, I need to establish the broader context for what happened next. Concurrently with my letter, I was having yet another disciplinary issue with some boys in the group. Before I continue, I need to establish the broader context of my being uptight with the boys.

First, I was a paranoid jerk. When I first arrived at the church, I had let myself be bullied by two older men who constantly complained about the behavior of the youth. "Look what your youth did. They changed the numbers on the attendance board." (According to the sliding letters/numbers sign outside our sanctuary, the preceding Sunday our Sunday school attendance had been 3000 and our offering was larger than the gross domestic product of several Caribbean nations.) "I work hard on the board, and I don't appreciate them doing that." Or: "During your lock-in" (an overnight sleepover in the church) "your youth broke the coffee pot in the Golden Ager's Sunday school room." Or: "Your youth discharged one of the fire extinguishers downstairs."

Before I continue, I need to explain how I finally improved my relations with the Brothers Grim in Christ. It took several years. The first breakthrough happened when one of them came into my Sunday school class and bawled me out in front of the kids. He was fussing at me for graphically describing side effects of chemotherapy during a seminar I had been asked to lead on hospital visitation. He told me he wanted to "puke all over [me]." He turned and walked away. I followed him out and called his name. He whipped around, and I got toe to toe with him. "Do you see that door right there?" I asked, pointing at my office.

"Yeah."

"The next time you have a problem with me: call me, make an appointment, and come in there and talk to me. But don't ever take that tone of voice with me in front of my kids again." (Interesting. I just realized that while I resented it when the Brothers Grim in Christ said "your youth," I frequently referred to them as "my kids." I think in my case it was a term of endearment; with them it was a term of derision.) The man glared at me in rage overcome with shock.

Between Sunday school and worship, the lay person who directed our morning programs approached me and said with a chuckle, "Boy howdy, [Mr. Dyspeptic] is *mad at you.*"

"He'll get over it," I said flatly, calmed by the comfort of knowing my pastor would back me up 100%. My pastor had had his own run-ins with both the Brothers Grim in Christ. I knew my course of action. I would wait two weeks, then invite Mr. D.S. Peptic to play tennis. I did. He accepted. We had a rollicking great time and never had another cross word.

I took a while longer with Mr. Dyspeptic's half-brother, Mr. B.N. Charge. I had to be more careful with Mr. Charge; he was nice enough around folks his own age to have been elected a deacon. It was Mr. Charge who castigated me because of the statistics sign, the fire extinguishers, and the coffeepot—all victims of *my youth*. Granted, the fire extinguisher episode was a pretty significant issue. It caused a huge mess, was expensive, and, most importantly, was dangerous since a purged fire extinguisher offers little help in the event of a fire. I could even understand bringing the coffeepot to my attention—just not in the harsh way Mr. Charge did it. The thing was, I would find out a few years later, while telling these anecdotes to a youth member's parent, that *my youth* were guilty of none of the crimes. But I'll come back to that.

Once I went toe-to-toe with Mr. Charge—as I had done with Mr. Peptic—I came to believe that some men just will not respect a younger man until they see him stand up to them. With Mr. Charge I had waited until my pastor retired. While I had known my pastor would back me up with Mr. Peptic, I knew Mr. Charge was a horse's cousin of a different color. While—in the sanctity of his office—my pastor would refer to any number of members, Mr. Charge included, as beasts of burden who may have borne our savior into Jerusalem on Palm Sunday, the fact was, Mr. Charge carried the money bags.

It just so happened, though, that right after our pastor retired, Mr. Charge rotated off the deacon board. He wouldn't be eligible for three years, and I was feeling more secure in my own political clout. It also occurs to me that having survived the controversy this is all building up to, I may have felt somewhat invincible. (I'm not proud of any of this by the way. The details here are meant as descriptive not, prescriptive. While I believe it is necessary to stand up to folks sometimes, it could be done much better than the way I did.)

For years our sanctuary had been easily confused with a walk-in freezer. Mr. B.N. Charge's control of the church was expressed primarily through his sole access to the locked thermostat in the sanctuary. He believed that the body heat of the congregation would make the sanctuary too warm, so he set the thermostat somewhere in the sixties, ignoring the fact that a *thermostat* would react to rising temperature. For whatever reason, our pastor let Eskimo-man have his way. I, however, finally lost my patience. During morning worship one Sunday, I sat next to a visiting mother and her children. The mother was in a summer, sleeveless, lime green, jumper-style dress. I noticed when she crossed her arms that she was covered with goose pimples. I offered her my jacket; she declined; I insisted, and she gratefully accepted. As the final hymn was being sung, she returned my blazer. When the pastor began his benediction, I was slipping out the side door to my station to shake hands with departing worshippers. As I stepped through the door I encountered Mr. Charge. I motioned for him to look through the door that I held slightly ajar. "Look at that woman on the second row," I said. He looked, then I shut the door. With a sneer I asked, "What was she doing?"

"It looked like she was shivering," he said in amazement.

"Yes. She is shivering because it is cold enough to hang meat in there," I said. "Now when this service is over, set that thermostat on 72 and don't ever touch it again, or I'll break that glass cover off of it and set it myself."

To my amazement he said, "OK."

Whoa! I had gone toe-to-toe with Mr. Charge. I was emboldened. I felt a new power. But it was the unwieldy power of flooding wet-weather gulch, and the next encounter with Mr. Charge, I let the water out of its banks.

Our pastor had retired, meaning the one external governor of my fury with Mr. Charge was now gone. A few short weeks after our pastor's departure, I was standing in the hallway waiting to process into worship. The choir filed from the choir room and waited for the music minister to emerge and give them the cue to enter. I happened to notice Mr. Charge striding down the hall, sneering, slapping his rolled up bulletin against his palm. Our minister of music emerged from the choir room. Bulging his eyes at the minister of music, and using the index finger of his right hand, Mr. Charge thumped the face of his watch. (The face of the watch was on the palm side of his wrist, a practice that annoyed me.) After a few emphatic thumps on the watch, he jabbed his finger toward the sanctuary and said, "Let's go! Get in there."

I waited until the choir had processed in so there would be no witnesses. "B.N.!" I said, sticking my face in his so suddenly and closely that he was startled and started backing up. I pursued until he was backed into the wall. "Do you know how hard it is to lead *worship* when you have just been jawed at? I have *had it!* If you need to complain about something, you come by the office on Monday morning. But complaining to us about *anything* right before we go into worship stops today! Are we clear!?

B.N. was smiling. He had his hands up. "OK."

"Sam knows what time it is, and he knows when the choir is ready to go. Now you leave him alone and let him do his job." I narrowed my eyes at him one more time for good measure.

"OK," he said with an embarrassed smile.

"Thank you."

The remainder of my tenure, Mr. Charge treated me like a son—a good son. In retrospect, I deeply regret the manner in which I took my stands with these two fine men. I could have accomplished the same thing with a still firm but more civil, Christ-like tongue. True, Jesus scourged the temple, but these men were no money changers, just curmudgeons. But I also learned that they did not respect me until I stood up to them.

Early on, though, I accepted Mr. Charge's criticism—and his accusations. Then, one day, I happened to describe some of our run-ins to a mother of one of the younger youth members.

"Oh, no," she said with a blush when I told her about the sign-pilfering incident. "Our young adult Sunday school class used to do that. The sign was right next to our class. B.N. would change the numbers about half way through Sunday school. That would be our cue to refill our coffee cups... and change the sign."

Speaking of coffee cups, I told her about the coffeepot incident.

"Oh, no. I remember that night. I was chaperoning and I brought Michael with me. He would have been in about... third grade?...then. He broke that coffeepot. I meant to tell you. I guess I forgot. I'm sorry."

"Now all you have to tell me is Michael set off the fire extinguisher in the preschool department."

Her eyes widened, she blushed, and lowered her head bashfully.

"No!"

"He had to get up on a chair to do it. But he did it."

"Oh, man! I tongue-lashed the youth group that night!"

I thought back on that night. I remembered that at the outset of my scolding lecture I was given a moment's pause just after I described the infraction. Daniel, one of the older youth blurted out, "That was so...." From the tone of his voice, it sounded like he was about to say "That was so Franky," or "...so Johnny" or any number of his peers. I passed it off that he was probably going to say, "That was so wrong." Besides, I didn't want him to rat out one of his peers over this, and, frankly, I didn't want to know who it was, since I was assuming it was one of *my youth* and I didn't want the headache of having to deal with the parents to whom I would have to report the incident. Now, as I thought back on that night, I was filled with admiration for Daniel. He could have ratted out Michael with no fear of any negative outcomes from his peers. If anything he would have been lionized for taking the heat off the group and placing it on the pesky Michael. Instead, he quickly sized up the situation and decided that after my lecture the matter would be closed, why subject Michael to whatever even worse consequences would befall him when his parents were told. But Daniel's nobility was for naught; Michael's mother had found out anyway.

I didn't ask her how she found out. I was already too busy kicking myself for letting Mr. Charge influence my attitude toward *my youth*. I had accepted Mr. Charge's criticisms as a reflection of the will of the church. I had been so afraid that the adults would see me as not having control over the youth, so afraid that I would be seen as an ineffective babysitter rather than a *leader*, so paranoid that the powers that be would take my job... that I took on the air of battleship commander who would impress the brass at the Pentagon with my running of a tight ship.

So, I often was a short-tempered, harsh jerk. But I also passionately cared for and wanted the best for our church's youth. The problem with being a short-tempered, harsh jerk is that when you do take a legitimate stand, it may be mistaken for just another example of harshness.

Thus, when I asked a disruptive youth to leave a class, it led to a confrontation with the parents who felt I was being too harsh. Many of the other parents, upset with my criticism of their children's clothing, were eager to hear and accept any criticism of me. The complaints of my handling of the one situation merged with the other. A group of parents asked for a meeting with me. I would find out later that my pastor made sure some parents would be there to prevent me from being unfairly attacked.

The meeting was scheduled to follow the evening service after "youth Sunday," the annual day that youth led the worship services. Before the evening service, a supportive father sidled up next to me and whispered, "You're a good man. I've got your back." I had never been called a man before; I stood up a little straighter and thanked him. Then after the service, another member said it was the best youth Sunday the church had had in 20 years. It was the best of times it was the worst of times. The guillotine was yet to come.

I walked into the meeting, trying to appear confident. I walked to the front of the room and, without speaking, picked up a white board marker and wrote four words on the board: Then I turned to the assembly.

"I once had a teacher who said that these are the four tasks of a minister." I turned and pointed to each. "We are to guide, sustain, heal, and reconcile. Because we are Baptists, we affirm the priesthood of every believer. I had another teacher who told me that the doctrine of the priesthood of the believer does not mean that we are each Lone Rangers; we are priests to each other. Since we are all ministers to each other, I want everything said here tonight to be intended to guide, sustain, heal, and reconcile."

One parent cut right to her issue. "Brad, I know you mean well, but what right do you have to tell our children what to wear?"

I turned to a TV and pushed play on the VCR. I had cued the film *Ice Storm* to the scene where a middle school boy standing on the back row of a school orchestra is ogling down at the buttocks of a girl sitting in front of him wearing low cut pants and a midriff baring top.

I had barely turned from pushing the stop button before a father said, "What is the name of that movie. I don't want my kids to see it."

"Then don't let your children come to this church, because when they come into this room, that's what they see." I let that statement settle into every crevice of the room and resolved to see who would break the silence.

It was the mother of one of the routine mooners. "Brad, the problem is that you are singling out the girls. It is not fair."

I nodded pensively, raising my eyebrows, contemplating the accusation. "Tell you what. I'm going to describe a true event, and I want you to tell me what you think about how I handled it.

"When I first came here, Big Johnson t-shirts were all the rage. You all do know what Big Johnson t-shirts are, right?" Almost every head was shaking.

"OK. Let me describe one. Shortly after I came here as youth minister, we were involved in a youth co-ed flag football league. One Sunday afternoon, I showed up for a game and one of our young men was wearing a Big Johnson t-shirt. "Big Johnson" is a euphemism for penis. This line of t-shirts uses Big Johnson as a trade name for a fictitious line of products. Like a motorcycle. That t-shirt had a buxom female straddling a motorcycle. The shirt said something like 'Always have a Big Johnson between your legs.' The shirt being worn at our flag football game showed a young couple with their head and feet sticking out of each end of a pup tent. The roof of the tent showed the distinct outline of an erect penis. The shirt said, 'Big Johnson Pup Tents... Don't go to the woods without your Big Johnson.'

"Now, how many of you want your daughters playing co-ed flag football with a boy wearing that shirt?"

No one budged or blinked.

"Come on. Raise your hand if you think it's OK for that shirt to be worn at a church function."

A slow exposure picture would not have had a single blur.

"Do you want to know what I did?"

I waited for a few heads to nod.

"I was prepared for such an event. I approached the boy and said, 'That shirt is not appropriate. You have two choices. You can change into a shirt I have in my car or you can go home.' He looked down at his shirt and said, 'Oh gosh! I forgot I had this on. Yeah, may I borrow a shirt.'"

"Now, do you all agree with the way I handled that?"

Again, complete stillness.

"That wasn't a rhetorical question. I want you to raise your hand if that is the way you want your youth minister to handle that kind of situation."

Every person raised a hand.

"OK. I am not picking on your daughters. I have addressed clothing issues with our young men. The difference is, they have complied. 'What right do I have to address the issue.' I have the right because part of what you expect me to do is keep your children safe. When we go on trips, you want to know that they will come home." I narrowed my eyes in earnestness, not spite. "You entrust me with the lives and well-being of your children, and I take that *very* seriously." I gestured to the TV. "That kind of attire contributes to an unwholesome *and* un*safe* environment."

I was letting that sink in when a set of parents entered the room. If I had been strapped in an electric chair, they—the mother in particular—would have been there to throw the switch. They explained that they had been waiting in another room (the gas chamber?), thinking it had been the announced location of the meeting. After they were seated (arms crossed, scowling), one of my pastor-assigned guardian angels spoke up—but not merely because she was encouraged to by our pastor.

"Like many of you, when I got the letter, I was offended, and I thought Brad and [the pastor] were off base. Brad doesn't know this, but something he asked me a few days ago changed my mind. We were at a multi-church youth function; our kids were there with several other churches. At one point Brad nodded toward a girl sitting on the floor near us. Her pants were very low in the back, and you could see her… bottom.

Brad asked me if I found that offensive, and I said no. He said, 'really?' and I said, 'No, I don't.' He said 'OK' and walked away. But what he doesn't know is that I spent the rest of the evening watching that young woman. I saw a guy notice... the view. Then he actually went and got some of his friends. They came over and stood behind her, looking down her pants, snickering at each other, bobbing their eyebrows, and, you know, looking at her like a piece of meat. And I asked myself. 'Do I want boys looking at my daughter that way.' And I thought, no, no I don't.' And now I have a new respect for how much Brad cares about our children."

"I have to echo that," another voice came. It was Frieda, one of the last people I would have expected to hear speaking from that side of the issue. Her daughter regularly came to church dressed more closely to the day she was born than the day of her baptism. "I was *very* angry when I got the letter. And I was complaining about it pretty loudly to Mary and John about it. They looked at each other awkwardly and then Mary said, 'We've never said anything, but we've been concerned about how Missy dresses.' Then John said, 'I've been embarrassed sometimes when she has run up and hugged me. I wasn't sure where to put my hands. People would be watching, and I felt like I couldn't look at her because everywhere I looked I saw more skin than clothes." Frieda looked at me apologetically but addressed the group. "So, yes, I was upset at first, but I've asked other people if they felt like John and Mary, and I've come to find that Brad has told us what everybody else was afraid to say."

The late-arriving mothers did not like the course the meeting was taking. Nostrils flaring, eyes piercing through me, voice just barely below a shout, she said, "Well! *I'M* not so concerned about the clothing issue. *I* think there is a MUCH more important issue." (Everyone in the room looked at each other nervously, and I could see what they were thinking: *Uh-oh the most volatile person in this church was not here to hear the ground rules that everything we would say would be for the purpose of guiding, sustaining, healing, and reconciling.*) "*I* think it is essential for our youth to be able to trust their youth minister.  AND OUR CHILDREN (her voice cracked into a melodramatic sob followed by a venomous accusation) cannot... trust you... to KEEP THEIR CONFIDENCES."

I might have been angry if the accusation had not been so outrageous.  I would go to jail if a judge ordered me to break a confidence I believed I was ethically bound to keep.  However, for a split instant I computed that if her accusation snowballed, I would not be able to defend myself.  I had revealed a confidence about her daughter— because I was legally *and* ethically bound to do so.  In fact, when her daughter had told me that her stepfather had burned her with a cigarette, and I told her "You know I have to report this," she had said, 'That's what I want you to do." But I would not be able to tell this important detail to the group.  Just as I could not defend myself for not testifying on behalf of a popular church member in a custody battle; I could not tell people what I knew that would prevent me from taking an oath and endorsing visitation rights for a person who had confessed (in a slightly drunken state) to having recently threatened her child with physical harm.  Now, here I was again, like Jimmy Stewart in *The Man Who Knew too Much*.  I couldn't say what I knew. Fortunately, I didn't have to."

"Now wait just a second," another mother said.  "You may disagree with Brad, but you cannot say he is not trustworthy.  I know that my children have shared things with Brad that they wouldn't tell me.  And I will admit that I've tried to milk him for information, but he hasn't told me. I trust him completely, and I know my children do too.  Every head in the room but two was nodding emphatically.  One of the two heads not nodding was afraid it would get slapped when its wife got it home.

"WELL!" the first mother said with the tone of a 7th grade girl in a playground argument, "that has not been my experience."

I let the venom in her voice serve as the broth for her to stew in. The group was beginning to get the flavor of the hostility with which I was dealing. This mother's misplaced rage had just done more for me than any positive endorsement. She had just made me a wounded martyr. I could see the group's anger with me begin to dissolve.

Still, there were legitimate concerns about my temper and harshness. The meeting went on for two more hours. Midway through, a father got up and went to check on the youth who were outside playing in the parking lot. When he came back, he waited for a lull in the conversation, then reported. "I just went to check on the kids. When I walked out the door they swarmed around me. All they asked was, 'Is Brad OK?' They are worried to death about him and that they have gotten him in trouble."

Finally, the mother who had called the meeting claimed the floor. She began crying as she described my asking her child to leave Sunday school. I carried a box of Kleenex across the room to her. Actually, it was not that I had asked her son to leave; it was that I had called him a name in the process. I emphatically denied this. But after several minutes it became apparent it was of no use to deny it. So I said, "OK. While I don't remember calling him a jerk, I will grant that I have said things in the past that I don't remember saying. So let's assume I did call your son a jerk. What did I do within an hour after church was over?" She shook her head. "Did I not call and apologize? What I remember is that I called and said that I did not regret asking him to leave, but I did regret *how* I asked him to leave. Is that not the case?" The mother tearfully nodded. "I understand that you were mad at me. I understand why you are still mad at me. Saying 'I'm sorry' doesn't take away the hurt. But I have apologized as best I know how." Then, with tears coming to my eyes, I asked, "What do I need to do so that we can be at peace?"

Sniffling, she shrugged. "I think our meeting tonight has let me see your true heart."

The next morning my phone rang before I left to go to work. "Brad. This is Angela." Angela had never volunteered to help with *anything*. She had shown up as moral support for one of her angry friends and to see the fireworks. In my mind's eye I saw a time-lapsed image of her posture the night before. At the beginning of the meeting she was shoulder to shoulder with another mother, arms crossed, scowling. Half way through the meeting she physically scooted away from her friend. By the end of the meeting she was looking at her friend with eyes that said, "You left out a lot of details of your story."

"I have four things I need to say to you," Angela began. "First, I could not have done what you did last night. We raked you over the coals for three hours, and you were a complete gentleman. Second, I should not have listened to just one side of the story in the first place. Third, I had no right to be there since I've never showed up for anything else. So fourth, if you ever need *anything*, a chaperone for a trip, a lock-in, *anything*, you call *me*."

I thanked Angela emphatically for her call. I told her I appreciated her affirming my being a gentleman and that I believed it took a noble heart for her to admit her mistakes and take the initiative to call. I told her that I often argue with my wife, but when we worked through our rifts it would strengthen our relationship, and I was sure that this struggle in our church family would only make us stronger.

Arriving at my office I found a bouquet of balloons from one of my most ardent supporters and active volunteers. The bouquet was weighted to my desk with a large glue stick. The attached card said, "We tore you to pieces last night. If this doesn't get you back together, there's more where this came from."

**Question for Reflection**
>A wide variety of opinions and levels of comfort regarding what constitutes appropriate dress exists in the church. How do we strike the balance between having standards and being accepting and welcoming?

# CHAPTER 14

## As Uno with Authoritatis

THEY WERE THE EPITOME OF BOREDOM. As the chaplain assigned to the hospital's geriatric rehabilitation unit, I was required to attend the unit's weekly rounds, the meeting where each department reported on the status of each patient. The meeting was chaired by the unit's physician, Dr. Halston, a man with the size, swagger, and wardrobe of a Mafia don. Attendants at the cabal were the head nurse (long-time veteran, mother of 3), psychiatrist (arch nemesis of the physician), physical therapist (tall, handsome young man), occupational therapist (athletic female), speech therapist (bombshell blond), and chaplain (unit mascot).

All the other departments' personnel had clinical-sounding things or Latin abbreviations to report.

"Nursing?"

"Mrs. Smithers' blood pressure continues to decrease with a daily range from 140 over 90 to 150 over 95." Blah blah blah.

"Psychiatry?"

"Mrs. Smithers is oriented times four. Her cognition and speech is lucid. Her depression inventory score is 10 points lower than last week but still in the mildly depressed range. She reports marked decrease in tearfulness since attending group therapy." Blah blah blah.

"Physical therapy?"

"Mrs. Smithers' has 50% lateral shoulder movement. Left hand grip is 10 pounds. Right hand grip is 22 pounds. Continuing manual manipulations B-I-D." Blah blah blah.

"Occupational therapy?"

"Mrs. Smithers successfully negotiated personal hygiene exercises. She completed 80% of household chore tasks but was not successful with basic food preparation tasks." Blah blah blah.

"Speech?"

"Mrs. Smithers continues to struggle differentiating the b-r and b-l diphthongs." Blah blah blah.

"Chaplain?"

Usually I just shook my head. Due to the grueling daily schedule on the rehab unit, if patients weren't in some type of therapy session, they were so worn out they were sleeping. Since coronary patients spent most of their time lying in bed and wanted someone to talk with, I spent most of my time on that unit. I only had contact on the geriatric rehab unit with those two or three patients who came to the weekly unit worship service or if a patient requested a visit. Mrs. Smithers was someone who had requested a visit. I actually knew something about her. And it might even inform her continued level of depression and anxiety. But I needed to give this report in the official, clinical-sounding terminology of the rest of the treatment team.

"I met with Mrs. Smithers for approximately 15 minutes. Three times she expressed concern about her status post death."

The unit physician's eyes looked to one side. The emperor was wearing his new clothes, and he wondered what everyone else thought of them. Was "status post death" a phrase he should know? Did he admit in front on his treatment team— in front of Dr. Sigmund— that *he* was not aware of the importance of a patient's *status post death*? Everyone around the table was wondering the same thing, but not letting on, admiring the emperor's new clothes.

Finally, Dr. Halston ventured to ask, "What do you mean by that?"

Not "What does *that* mean." That would have meant there was something he didn't know. "What do *you* mean by that?" If there was something unclear, the problem lay with me. He was right. But, in my defense, I was just following an edict of my upbringing. Every time I entered the kitchen of my childhood I had passed under a plaque that said, "If you can't dazzle them with brilliance, baffle them with bull." (The plaque was written in gothic letters with the "B" in "bull" capitalized, so the play on our last name was clear.)

Feeling sheepish, but trying to sound matter-of-fact, I translated my obfuscation into the vernacular— the plain, ordinary, I'm-just-a-minister vernacular. "She's worried about whether or not she's going to heaven or hell when she dies."

Dr. Halston nodded sagely. Of course.

There was a brief awkward pause. What should his follow-up question be? I didn't want to get on his bad side, so I didn't wait for him to find one. "I will continue to meet with her and explore her spiritual concerns."

"Thank you, Brad." He closed Mrs. Smither's chart, and the head nurse handed him the next one in the stack. The eyes in the room went off me. My skeleton held my body's image in the chair. My soul sank six floors down into the flaming bowels of my supervisor's office. When my body caught up with it the next day in case review, I confessed my idiotic insecurity and how my attempt at sounding important had blown up in my face. My supervisor laughed compassionately, admiring my honesty. He then challenged me to think about the importance of spiritual care and pushed me to consider why it was I who was selling short my value as a member of the medical team. Then one of my peers shared an anecdote he had just read in Lewis Grizzard's autobiography. Grizzard, a syndicated columnist with the *Atlanta Constitution*, was describing his experience with open heart surgery. He spoke of his predilection for wine, women, and song and of confessing his sins to a chaplain, then receiving a hug from the chaplain. He described the liberating feeling of a non-condemning hug from a minister of God. I thought about that. Grizzard was grateful for the physician who repaired his heart *and* for the minister who helped him experience the presence and redemption of the Great Physician. Maybe I did have something to offer.

My new-found confidence came in handy at my next staff meeting. But before I describe my liberation, I probably need to describe an event that had contributed to my insecurity in the clinical setting.

For an assignment I had written a description of when nursing staff might call upon chaplains for a consultation with patients. I described phrases that might discretely hint at spiritual concerns. ("I'm wondering why this happened to me.") I suggested that chaplains should not only be called for emotional and spiritual crises. Special occasions such as anniversaries, birthdays, and good medical news, would be a time to let the chaplain know to come and celebrate with a patient. My supervisor was so impressed he added my paper to the intern orientation notebook. He also nominated me to present my paper when a unit nurse asked him to suggest an in-service training topic for her staff.

I was thrilled. I envisioned wide-eyed nurses enthralled with my remarks, surrounding me at the end of the session, ooing and ahhing with "Why didn't I ever think of that? I feel like a better nurse now."

With visions of sugar plums dancing in my head, I strode into what I believed was the Coronary Care Unit. It wasn't the way I remembered it. Chairs were arranged in two rows of six. A gavel pounded and the bailiff called "Hear ye, hear ye, this in-service training is now in session." With that I took the stand before a jury of twelve peerless persons, all of whom had been sequestered for weeks with only bread and water. I stood before them— a caught-red-handed axe murderer and hard evidence of my also being a telemarketer. Sentencing me was the only thing that stood between them and being home with their families for Christmas.

Arms crossed. Jaws set. Eyes knifing. *Who is this punk kid, trying to tell me how to be a nurse?*

I got rattled. I muddled my way through. When I was done, the entire staff bolted for the door without a word. *Guilty. Crucify him.*

The head nurse and her assistant compassionately gave me my last meal: a sugar cookie and a glass of weak powdered lemonade. Then, my confidence, having betrayed me, went out and hanged itself.

In an effort to resurrect it, I had thought that maybe using a fancy, clinical-sounding terminology would gain me respect. That had backfired, too. But hearing the great Lewis Grizzard's praise for his chaplain helped resuscitate belief in my own purpose.

I also came to realize that sometimes it helps to fight fire with fire. If you need to advocate for a patient or family, and clinicians like clinical language, use their language. Just make sure it is *their* language and not your own language simply spoken in their accent.

It was a general medicine unit's case review meeting. Unlike on the rehab unit, I had a great deal of interaction with the patients on this unit. For a two week stretch, one of my patients was Mickey, a man in his 30s who was living at home with his parents. I met his mother, who looked like she had posed for *American Gothic*. I suspected when I met her husband he would be holding a pitchfork at his side. While the mother was talking, the son looked at me with contempt. At my second visit, the son was alone in the room. He told me he was gay and HIV positive.

"You think I'm scum, don't you?" Mickey said.

"You think, because I'm a chaplain, I'm a Bible-thumping, gay-bashing bigot. Right?"

"Are you?"

"Maybe." He looked both surprised by—and wary of—my candor. "I like to think of myself as unprejudiced." I laughed nostalgically. "When I was about five or six years old, I was living in Augusta, Georgia. One day we were visiting a neighbor. Their son was playing in the dirt and was blackened from head to toe. Repeating a word I likely heard at school, I said, 'You look like a nigger!' When we got in the car, my dad turned, sternly looked at me in the back seat and said, 'When we get home, you're getting a spanking.' I thought, *What did I do?* My mother said, 'Now, hon. He doesn't know what that means. We just need to explain to him.' I thought, *Yeah, Dad, Mom's right. Whatever it is, explain it. No spanking necessary.* Mickey grinned ever so slightly. I continued my story. "Dad then explained about slavery, the Civil War, and the nature of the word *nigger* as a term of hate. I was cool with not using the word. I hadn't known it was a word of hate. It's just what I had heard people with black skin called. I remember thinking, *Gosh, I'm glad Dad is telling me this. I don't want to be mean or say mean things.*" I sighed. "And I've always tried not to be prejudiced. But let's face it, we've all got our prejudices." I paused. "Look, I'll shoot straight with you. When I went to seminary I read a lot of stuff and heard a lot of people argue about homosexuality. I'd hear the argument on one side and say 'Yeah.' Then I'd hear the argument on the other side and say, 'Yeah.' Honestly, I don't know what I think. One minute I'm convinced it's a sin; the next I think any prohibition in scripture is either a misinterpretation or rooted in the cultural context of the writers. Right now I do lean toward the 'it's a sin'-but-I'm a sinner, too" position. On the other hand, maybe it's like the whole issue with slavery. A hundred years ago, and even less, it was preachers who were saying the Bible protected people's rights to have slaves. Now you couldn't find a handful of American preachers who would agree that slavery is OK. And I am scared to death when I wonder what people fifty years from now will think about me now. If I'm alive, I wonder what *I* will think of my position now." I paused again. "So could we agree on this: we're both trying to find God's will. You may be right; I may be right. But regardless of right or wrong, we can be sure that we're both human beings. And if we're both human beings making an honest effort to do the right thing, then we owe each other respect. And come to think of it, while as your chaplain I want to help you, I think *you* can help *me*. Even if I do think homosexual behavior is sinful, I don't want to come off as a bigot about it. So can we make a deal that we'll both keep honestly searching and treat one another as human beings and that you'll let me know if you feel treated less than a human being?"

Slowly Mickey started nodding. He still looked wary, but he said, "deal."

"Would you like to pray together?"

He thought for a moment. "OK."

I offered my hand. He took it. We prayed.

That week during unit rounds, Mickey and his family were the focus of discussion. The social worker expressed concerns about Mickey's relationship with his parents. A male nurse spoke up. "Oh God, you're right. His mother is so controlling." He spoke in defense of Mickey, but it sounded like he was defending himself from his own parents as well. "The other day she told me that she was worried about Mickey coming home because he would never *obey* her. She actually said he wouldn't *obey* her. I mean, he is a grown man and his mother is talking about him like a child. She is *so* controlling."

While the mother did seem Puritanical and ashamed of her son's homosexuality, she also struck me as loving him dearly and being concerned for his wellbeing. The tenor of the staff toward the mother seemed excessively hostile and more likely to exacerbate the problem rather than help the family deal with their issues constructively. I spoke up.

"I'm not sure the issue is that she's overly controlling. I mean, don't we ourselves here in the hospital complain when patients don't follow the instructions we give them? The only difference is that we say 'the patient is non-compliant with protocol.' We *say* 'the patient is non-compliant with protocol' but what we *mean* is that the patient won't *obey* us. So maybe the issue is not that Mrs. Wood is controlling. Maybe the issue is that she just doesn't have a vocabulary as sophisticated as ours to express her legitimate frustrations with his refusal to take his medications or exercise."

The room fell silent. Everyone in the room but one person had looks on their faces that said, "Wow. That was profound." The other person, the nurse who was so adamant— probably about being a single male feeling controlled by his own mother— was looking at me with a stumped stare. Wheels were turning behind his eyes as he struggled unsuccessfully for a counter argument. He refused to concede. Instead of raising his eyebrows to say *hmm, interesting* like everyone else, he pursed his lips and furrowed his eyebrows at me to say *Bible-thumper*.

The challenge of any leadership position is finding the balance between allowing power to corrupt on one extreme or being indecisive and ineffective on the other. However, even when the cowboy is acting in good faith, there is no guarantee that the horses being led to water will want to drink.

When he was a boy, the religious leaders in the temple were impressed that Jesus "spoke as one with authority." He knew his stuff. But later, people still wanted to crucify him. He knew how to balance power and humility. He uttered a word and demons fled or storms were stilled.

On the other hand, in the face of outrageous allegations, Jesus impressed the judge by remaining silent.

When I was an intern chaplain, my supervisor constantly challenged me with the issue of pastoral authority. When I wrote a maudlin letter to an abusive physician, before sending it, I showed it to my supervisor. He said I gave up too much of my power; I put the doctor on a pedestal. "What does my name plate on the door say?" he asked me.

"Dr. Samuel Houston."

"Do you know what the doctors call me?"

"Sam?"

"Yeah. Even though I have a doctorate in my field, they call me by my first name. And when they call me 'Sam,' I call them by their first name. Some of them do a double take the first time that happens. But when they come to me with a problem, they come to me as a fellow professional, not as a subordinate."

Wow. Would I ever have the wherewithal to be that assertive? I had stood up to a doctor when he was verbally abusing another employee, but that was before I knew what a risky thing I was doing.

Another time I told one of my supervisors that I didn't feel comfortable probing the concerns of a patient with family members sitting in the room. No matter when I went by, someone was always there. "What might happen if you asked if you could speak with him privately?" my supervisor asked.

"I... I don't... I guess... ."

"Don't doctors and nurses sometimes ask visitors to leave the room in order to do an examination?"

"Yes."

"Is what you have to do any less important?"

"OK. Point well taken. It's just... . Gee. I don't know."

Would I ever have the sense of appropriate confidence and power to ask to be alone? Yes I would, but it would happen in a living room, not a hospital room.

Due to a physical disability of one of their members, the Windsor family asked me to see them therapeutically in their home. They even offered to pay me for the extra mileage and time spent commuting to their house from the counseling center where I worked. It was a four generation family. Gramma, the father's mother, was wheel chair bound, and had been living with her son's family since the death of her husband one year before. Father, Rex, was a stock broker; mother, Mary, was a nurse. Their oldest daughter was a social worker in another city. Their youngest daughter, Dianna, age twenty-four, worked as an assistant to a local interior designer and lived with her husband in an apartment a few miles from her parents.

The mother and father originally contacted me about helping his mother deal with her grief. Mid-way through the first session, it was apparent their greatest concern was for their youngest daughter. The parents had begun keeping their infant grandson on occasional weekends when the daughter was working out of town on a new hotel project. Gradually they were keeping him more and more on weeknights. But a chance encounter between the grandmother and her daughter's employer led to the discovery that the weekend hotel project had been completed months before. The grandmother had not confronted the daughter initially, thinking there might be a reasonable explanation and not wanting to appear suspicious. Then, on a Wednesday afternoon, the grandmother had stumbled on an opened credit card bill in the bottom of a diaper bag. The bill was for just over $8,000. The envelope was addressed to her daughter but at a post office box. The current bill listed $1,200 in charges at the casino in Cherokee, North Carolina, and nearly $500 in charges at a tavern that turned out to be in a rural section of a neighboring county. The grandmother noticed the charges were all on Monday, Tuesday, and Thursday evenings at the same times. The next evening, a Thursday, she was parked across the street from the tavern and saw her daughter park and enter the tavern alone. Her son-in-law was at work. She wondered where her grandson was. She crossed the street, prepared to make a scene. She imagined she would find her daughter standing with a beer in a back room at a slot machine. As she passed her daughter's car she saw that a blanket was thrown like a tent over the infant car seat. She had not wanted to think the unthinkable, but she took her own key to her daughter's car and let herself in.

She had burst into tears when she looked under the blanket and found her grandson. She extracted him, then started toward the tavern with him, planning to confront her daughter, babe in arms. A few steps from the door she had another idea. She had an infant carrier in her own car. She went back to her daughter's car, retrieved a pen and piece of paper from the glove box, wrote "How could you do this!!!? I took him HOME. –Mother".

The daughter had called her mother's cell phone ten minutes later. She had just needed to get out of the house; she was going to check on him every few minutes and leave if he woke up; several of her friends did the same thing.

The grandparents agreed to return the child only upon the daughter's promise of going to Gambler's Anonymous. These suspicions only grew worse with time. When the daughter showed up drunk to pick up her son, her parents refused to let her take the boy. They took her car keys. She walked home in a rage. She apologized the next day, said it would never happen again. She would go to Gambler's Anonymous. But the grandparents would not relent. They were going to keep their grandson with them.

The phone call from the grandmother came while I was in session with another client. After seeing the client to the door, the counseling center receptionist handed me the urgent phone message. I called the grandmother. She was on her way from work to the daycare to pick up her grandson. The daughter had gotten a court order for the grandparents to surrender the child to her custody. The son-in-law was going to be at the grandparents' house to take the child. He had called the police to make sure the grandparents did not flee with the child—like he had heard of grandparents doing on *America's Most Wanted*. The police had been waiting at the daycare and were following the grandmother as we spoke. "I cannot *believe* this is happening," she said. "I'm really worried about how Mom is going to react. Fortunately [my husband] is not going to be there, or the police might be needed. When I first called I was just panicking, and was wondering if you could come over and help me deal with Mother. But I'm sure you probably have clients."

"Actually, I just finished for the day. I'm on the way."

"Oh, thank you. We will, of course, pay you for a session."

Part of me started to say "don't worry about it." I still had twinges of guilt about being paid for intervening in an emotional crisis. Then, I remembered that my plumber didn't look guilty when he charged me $100 for a half-hour for what turned out to be a spoon stuck in the kitchen sink—and after he had evacuated the sink of water and debris and I could see the obstacle creating the clog, *I* had gotten the spoon out while the plumber had gone to his truck to get a tool. "Just concentrate on driving. I'll see you at your house."

It was just a few miles from the counseling center to the grandparents' house in an exclusive gated community. I arrived at the entrance just as Mrs. Windsor and the police turned in, coming from the opposite direction. I had been there enough that the guard smiled and waved. Pairs of mothers and strollers were out in force. *Great. As if things weren't bad enough, someone was going to see the police in the Windsor's driveway; local cell phone towers would be overwhelmed in minutes.*

The son-in-law was leaning against the front of his dented, kayak-and-bike-racked SUV, arms crossed, eyes nervous in the face of the reality he was creating. The police officers sheepishly got out of their cruiser. Mrs. Windsor gingerly lifted the baby from his car seat. The son-in-law came a few steps closer Mrs. Windsor hugged the baby and addressed the officers. "Before I do this, I want you to know that this is a mistake. His mother is an alcoholic. My grandson is safe here. You don't have to worry; I'm not going to cause a problem. I just want you to know that I love this child, and I only want to keep him safe."

The policemen smiled and nodded patronizingly. Mrs. Windsor kissed her grandson— who was old enough to be looking around, wide-eyed. Addressing her son-in-law, Mrs. Windsor said, "Perry, I know you're just doing what Martha asked you to do. But you know she's in no shape to take care of Timothy."

"She's doing just fine," Perry said, sounding like a boy defending a dog who had dug up the neighbor's garden.

Mrs. Windsor handed Timothy to his father. Perry accepted his son with the look of a powerhouse tennis player receiving a trophy after very narrowly defeating an injured underdog— relieved to win but knowing he didn't deserve the accolade. He nodded at the police officers who had seen enough domestic disputes to know they were no longer needed, said goodbye, saddled back up in their squad car and rode off into the sunset.

If they had known who was driving the car they met half way down the block, they probably would have turned around and come back. I was watching Mrs. Windsor's eyes sadly watching the police drive away. Then her shoulders sank with her eyelids and she mouthed the words "Oh, no." I turned and saw Mr. Windsor arriving home early (he had forgotten his racquetball bag that morning). I believed I knew him well enough to know he would not resort to violence, but it would not surprise me if he saw his son-in-law, put two and two together, and used his car to block his exit. He didn't. He just glared at Perry with a look that said, "You idiot." He glanced at Mrs. Windsor with a *"How did you let this happen?"* look. "Were those police officers *here*?" he asked. Mrs. Windsor nodded. Scowling sarcastically at Perry and gesturing to an open exit, Mr. Windsor said, "Well, there you go. Take him home. We'll go in and call the funeral home and start making arrangements." Mrs. Windsor gasped a cry before her hand could stifle it; then she fled toward the house.

"Happy now?" Mr. Windsor condescended to Perry, shaking his head in disgust.

"I don't want to hurt nobody," Perry said with feigned resolve. "He's our son, and he needs to be with us."

"Alright. *Go.* Nobody's stopping you."

Like a school boy whose mother had threatened to whip him if he came home with grass stained pants, Perry said, "Martha told me to pick up the Pack-N-Play while I'm here."

"Fine!" Rex said, his face pulsing crimson, "I'll help you load it."

Inside, Rex's mother was sitting in her wheelchair like it was a throne, fingers interlaced on her lap. The matriarch pleasantly said, "Hi, Perry." She did not need to scold with either words or tone. If she had, it might have been easier for Perry to dislike her and take her great grandchild. But her quiet aplomb made it difficult to do anything of which she disapproved.

"Hi, Gramma," Perry said, his eyes filled with apology and pleading that she not require him to look her in the eyes. "How are you?" he asked perfunctorily.

"As well as a woman who should have died 10 years ago can be," she said with a smile, delivering her standard line. "How's work?"

"Good," Perry said, wide-eyed and robotic, his mind yearning for the portable crib to be brought, so he could make his escape.

From the upstairs Rex barked. "Perry! You're going to have to come show us how to break this thing down."

"Those things are so cantankerous," I said consolingly. "I'll come help.

"Thanks," Perry said, and began leading me to the spiral staircase.

I smiled at Gramma Windsor, who smiled back sagely, her eyes narrowing just perceptibly enough to say "fix this."

Upstairs, Perry led me down a hallway toward the bedroom that had been converted into a nursery. Rex looked ready to throw the crib out the window. Mary had dried her tears and was now stoic, obviously trying to calm Rex who was red-faced, drenched in sweat, and a prime candidate for a heart attack or stroke. Rex shot Perry a look that said, *see what kind of problems you're causing?* Perry responded by sheepishly but deftly breaking down the crib into a compact state that I had up to that point believed was never possible after the infernal things left the factory. Rex's face subtly betrayed his effort to hide his disappointment that Perry succeeded. Without a word we all filed out and back toward the downstairs.

Just as we arrived at the den the doorbell rang. It was Perry's mother and stepfather. I didn't have to look to the driveway to know she would be driving an eight-year-old Buick Regal or Cadillac, traded for the original that likely had been bought on an initial splurge after receiving a lump sum divorce settlement. Anyone could see that she likely spent more money per year on makeup, hair color, and designer pocketbooks than the gross domestic product of several island nations in Polynesia.

Twenty minutes later it was apparent that Perry was only going to take Timothy to save face. He was an adult, and he was not going to let his mother, stepfather, or in-laws tell him what to do. He had his arms crossed and was leaning against the wall, for all the world looking like a cliché regarding a cornered animal. The family was at an impasse but was not asking me for help. The parents seemed content to hurl accusations and derision at Perry. To the best of my knowledge, every single one of the accusations was true. But this was one type of truth that wasn't going to set anyone free.

Finally I spoke up. "I'd like to call timeout a minute. Do you all mind if Perry and I go for a walk outside?" I didn't ask Perry if he wanted to go outside. I wanted to get him out of the crossfire so he possibly could think in terms of his son rather than his own defensiveness. Rex threw up his hands. "Sure, whatever."

The parents stood in awkward silence as Perry and I walked toward the door. Just as the storm door was hissing shut behind me, I heard Mary ask Perry's parents, "Would you all like some tea?"

I allowed a few steps of silence, hoping the quiet would sink in and nurture Perry's appreciation for me and my rescue. I tried not to let my own awkwardness with the silence rush me into speaking. Finally, when instinct dictated that too much longer would be too much, I looked at Perry, cocked my eyebrow, shook my head once and said, "Whew. Quite a crossfire in there."

"Yeah," he said with stunned flatness, looking like a school boy of old leaving the principal's office after a sound paddling: too tough to cry but shocked by the intensity of the punishment the old codger had inflicted. After a brief pause he resolutely said, "But I gotta do what's best for Dianna and the baby. We are the parents and our child needs to be with us. My boss is letting us use one of his condos at the beach this weekend, and Dianna wants us to spend the weekend together. She wants us all to be together, so I'm bringing her our baby. I know Dianna has had a problem. She shouldn't have left the baby in the car while she went in a bar. But she has promised me nothing like that will happen again, and she ain't gonna drink no more."

"What if she does? What are you going to do?"

"Divorce her," Perry said with a definitive head bob.

Perfect. He had just opened the door. I allowed a long enough pause to create the appearance that I had to think of a response. "Who will take care of the baby then?"

"I will," Perry said with pitifully naïve defiance.

"I'm afraid not, Perry. As an objective outsider who's seen my share of custody battles, let me tell you what's going to happen." (We now had wandered well up into the back yard. I stopped walking and faced him. He glanced at me and then stared ahead.) "Given your employment history, your in-laws are going to sue for custody. Since you just said you would divorce her on the grounds of maternal incompetence, you're accepting that. Even if you have a good job at that point, if you take the baby today, all Rex and Mary will have to do is point to this day and tell the judge that you took your baby from a safe environment to one you yourself just admitted unstable— even downright unsafe. And I'm sorry to tell you, but the judge *will* grant custody to Rex and Mary." (Perry pursed his lips and subtly nodded in agreement.) "Now, if it were me? If I had a great set of in-laws like yours who were willing to provide *free* childcare for the weekend? I'd call my wife and prepare her for the fact that I wasn't coming home with the baby so she wouldn't fly into a rage when I got home empty-handed. I'd tell her something like 'You know what? I was almost to the car with the baby, and I thought-- *we've been under a lot of stress lately. I'd like to spend some time with just the two of us.*' Then I'd take my wife to that cabin in the mountains and make love until the cows come home!"

Perry, flatly staring at some unknown point, began ever so slightly nodding his head. "Alright," he finally said.

"Alright, what?"

"I'll leave him here."

"How are you going to do that?"

"I'll go back in there and tell them I want to leave the baby with them."

"Then what?"

"When the time is right this weekend, I'm going to tell Dianna I want her to take up our parents' offer to help pay for a few weeks at a rehab clinic."

"You want me to go with you, or you want to do it on your own."

"I'll do it."

"Perry," I said leaning my head to gain his eye contact. "Earlier in there you looked like a whipped school boy. Now you look like a man. I'll do anything I can to help you."

"Thanks," he said solemnly.

I got in my car and drove away as he headed back inside. I went back to my office to do some paperwork. Two hours later as I was leaving, Rex screeched to a stop in the parking lot. I saw the headlines on the next day's paper. "Local therapist gunned down outside clinic." I was wondering what had gone wrong and whether I should try to run around the building, quickly reasoning it would take too long to unlock the door. In my moment of hesitation Rex climbed from his car obviously empty handed. He strode toward me and finally in the gloaming light I saw that he was tearfully smiling. He threw his arms around me and hugged me. Then he stepped back, keeping his hands on my shoulders and through sobs said, "I don't know what you said, but I'll never forget you as long as I live."

The Windsors stopped seeing me in order to put all their financial resources into Dianna's residential treatment— in which they participated in conjoint family sessions. A few years later I ran into the entire clan Christmas shopping at a local mall the day after Thanksgiving. They greeted me enthusiastically. Dianna and Perry looked at me with grins that said the cows had come home many times in the intervening years. Our visit was brief as their handsome second-grader tugged on Dianna's arm, longing to move along to see Santa. Shaking her head with a smile, Dianna said "kids" looking at me and then her parents.

It was a subtle but nice way for Dianna to say "thank you" to her parents and me. Sometimes, subtle expressions of thanks sometimes are the best kind. The subtlety implies intimacy— that the thanks can only be understood because of a shared experience. But explicit thanks feels good, too. Like the appreciation once whispered to me at a wedding rehearsal dinner.

It happened toward the end of my eight-year tenure at the church I served as associate pastor after my one-year hospital residency in clinical pastoral education. But I was only beginning to use my shepherd's staff to guide with authority rather than simply for the appearance of competence.

I was performing premarital counseling for a teenage set of parents who had been referred to me by a former client. Due to turf wars between their families— each set of their parents had divorced and remarried, making a total of eight parents and stepparents— they wanted to have the wedding at a neutral site rather than one of their own churches. This decision was one of the many that made them— of the awfully-young-to-marry couples I had seen— one of the ones with the best heads on their shoulders.

Toward the end of our last session I asked if there was anything else they wanted to discuss. They looked at each other and smiled. "Actually there is," the bride said. "We love all our parents and stepparents. But they *hate* each other. They can't even be in the same room together." She sighed but smiled as she shook her head— looking more like the parent of some unruly children. "Billy and I want to have one big picture together on the stage at the front of the church. But we're afraid either they'll make a scene and refuse to stand next to each other, *or* they'll stand there with scowls on their faces. And I just want everybody to be happy and smile."

"Ah. Thank you so much for telling me. I'm glad I asked you." I nodded my head and looked at the two of them reassuringly. "I'll take care of that. But I'll need to meet with all of them. So before the rehearsal starts, I'll tell all of them I need to meet them in the choir room. OK?" The bride and groom looked at each other, nodded, then nodded at me.

So I did. I opened the side door to the sanctuary and said, "We'll begin the rehearsal shortly, but first I need to see all the parents and stepparents in the choir room please." There were a few nervous glances, but they complied.

They shuffled down the hall and into the choir room. They spread themselves across the room in a manner that a well-placed grenade would have caused only one or two casualties. But I was armed to the teeth with peace.

I perched on a stool front and center. A few of the women looked genuinely terrified. The men tried to look either stoic or snidely contemptuous of this minister who needed to get a real job; but I could see their blood pressure pulsing in their eyes. "I want to tell you one of the saddest stories I ever heard," I began. "A true story."

"For nearly 30 years, my father has directed graduation at the college where he teaches. The year after I graduated he called me and asked me if I remembered a certain gal who was a year behind me in school. 'Of course.' I said.

"Then Dad said, 'Today after graduation she was standing alone outside the stadium just sobbing. I asked her what was wrong.' She said 'My dad and stepmom are standing over there, and my mom and stepdad are standing over there, and I don't know which way to go!'"

I paused and let my salvo ricochet around the room. "Tomorrow is your children's day. They have told me that they want to have a family picture made with all of you in it and all of you smiling. Now I don't know the history between you. But whatever ill will you may have for one another is going to get left in here. I'll lock this room and you can come back and get it when the reception is over. But let me be clear. I am the officiant of this wedding. That means I'm something like a referee at a ballgame. And if I see a foul, I'm going to call it, and if necessary I'll throw you out of the game and send you to the locker room. The day I told my home church I wanted to become a minister, a former pastor called me. He gave me some advice and encouragement. Then he ended with a laugh: "and if you ever have a choice between a funeral and a wedding... take the funeral." The outlaw-inlaws before me snickered and began looking at each other. "I wondered what he meant. But I was just a teenager. As I began going to more weddings, I began to see what he meant. I have seen it all at weddings. I've seen everything from yelling matches to near fist fights. I've seen hair pulled. I saw one bride's brother spit in her face. Her face was still tear-stained in the wedding pictures."

I made firm eye contact with each person in the room. "I want you to know I will not tolerate it. If you cannot conduct yourself as an adult, this is the time for you to leave. But if you stay here once we walk out of this room, you are saying that you will be cordial; you will be respectful; and that tomorrow— even if you are standing next to someone you think is the spawn of Satan— you will smile the most genuine smile you have ever smiled. It is your children's day. I insist that you make sure they remember it fondly. If you can't do that, now is your time to slip out."

I looked around the room. The mother of the bride confidently broke the silence. "We'll be alright."

I raised my eyebrows. "Will we each be alright?" I looked at each person and they nodded their head in kind. I smiled. "Alright then. Let's go get these kids hitched and have fun doing it."

That night at the rehearsal dinner I was seated next to the mother of the bride. The room rang with peals of laughter. Opposite me sat the mother of the groom. Immediately beside her was her ex-husband's wife, the groom's stepmother. I knew this. An unknowing observer would have thought they were high school chums reunited at a class reunion. They laughed uncontrollably— even without the aid of alcohol at this tee-totaling dinner. At one point, the mother of the bride caught my attention. She subtly nodded toward the mother and stepmother of the groom who were engrossed in girlish conversation. I smiled and nodded at the mother of the bride. She leaned over and whispered, "Thank you for what you said. I think we all just needed to be reminded to be adults."

Don't we all? And just as making mature behavioral decisions is a never-ending personal process, using authority appropriately is a growth process, too. I left my clinical pastoral education newly convinced of the existence of ministerial authority. But I was a loose cannon. In a job interview after completing my Ph.D., a college dean asked me to give an example of one of my greatest mistakes. Without hesitating I said, "As an intern chaplain, I had a supervisor who kicked my tail. It was very much an in-your-face program. By the end of it, I realized how much I had needed someone to be in my face. I left the program very grateful for what it had done for me. Then I spent the first several years working in a church trying to run my youth group like a CPE program. I was very loving but also very much in the kids' faces. I tried to look wise for the sake of looking wise." I then told a shorter version of this encounter:

One day at church, a teenaged girl was in my office. As she told me about her problems, even though she had made no direct statements to the effect, I began to suspect her father was either an alcoholic or a drug addict. I remembered how my CPE supervisor had once written something about me down on paper, leaving me to wonder what he'd written. It had worked with me. Now this young woman sat before me, and if my guess about her father was right, secrecy was bred into her. If I asked her straight out, I might scare her away. I needed to be indirect. I had a tool in my bag and I wanted to use it; I wanted to impress her. 'I'll tell you what,' I said to the girl, pulling pen, paper, and an envelope from my desk. 'I think I know what's going on with you. I'm going to write it down on this piece of paper.' (I wrote down that I thought her father was either abusing alcohol or drugs. For good measure I also listed gambling and compulsive shopping.) 'Now. I'm going to seal this up in an envelope. Whenever you're ready to talk about it, we'll open this and see if I guessed right.' The young lady's face turned ashen with a look of almost terror. She left my office and never returned to our church. A few years later I saw her at her father's funeral. It was an overdose. It should have been a closed casket service.

The envelope stayed in the top drawer of my desk throughout the remainder of my tenure at the church. I kept it there to remind me how threatening misused authority can be. I kept it there to remind me that the shepherd's staff— according to the 23rd Psalm— should comfort the sheep and threaten only the wolves and lions.

This theme became an important aspect of my own therapy. During my Ph.D. program, I fell into the deepest depression of my life to that point. I began seeing a counselor at the university's student clinic. One day I told my counselor of a realization I had had.

"When I was in seminary, I worked as an aide in a psychiatric hospital. One night I was working on the adolescent unit. A fifteen-year-old girl became enraged for some reason. Her behavior was escalating toward violence. The other patients had been sent to their rooms, and the girl was pacing the dining area in a menacing way. One staff member was left to monitor her while the rest of the staff huddled to make assignments for the impending "physical management." The charge nurse gained consensus that, for the protection of the other patients and the girl herself, she would have to be taken forcibly to the seclusion room and placed in restraints. Four staff members were each assigned to a specific arm or leg of the girl. The charge nurse and a fifth staff member would apply the leather straps to her ankles, wrists, and abdomen— lashing them to the slots in the bed, fabricated for just that purpose. I was assigned to her head. This meant that I was to hold her head, to prevent her from head butting or biting. I had also been trained how to press the tips of my middle fingers into the nerve where the earlobe joins the upper jawbone. (If you do this you will see how intensely painful this can be even with mild pressure.) If necessary, sufficient pain was to be exerted to gain compliance without injury.

I don't remember the takedown. I only remember standing at the head of the bed, my hands over the girl's temples and ears, trying to hold her head still. Physically speaking, she was a fully grown woman. She was thrashing violently, creating the most difficult physical management I had ever experienced. Her long sandy hair was matted with sweat and tears and kept flying into her mouth. She would blow it out and then spit at me, screaming curses. The nurses' plan was to give her a tranquilizer via an injection that had to be placed in her thigh. This would require removing her jeans. This had to be done before the restraints were applied.

"NO!!!" The girl screamed. The nurse spread a sheet across her then reached under it and began unfastening the pants. "No! No! NO!!!!" *Dear God. What if she is a victim of sexual abuse. This is so doubly traumatic for her.* With unbelievable strength, she convulsed, lifting her legs and arms from the bed. Mind you, I could understand her moving the petite females, but the man to my right, pinioning her right arm, ran about six-feet, 220 pounds. She broke my hold easily and strained her neck in a nearly successful effort to bite my brawny co-worker's substantial arm. In the nick of time I grabbed her head, forced it back down, found the soft spot below her earlobe and applied pressure. She screamed— it seemed a scream more in the horror of being controlled than of pain. She screamed again when the needle pierced the side of her right hip.

The nurse and the fifth staff member began to apply the restraints. "Uh... Cathy?" the staff member asked. "Doesn't hospital policy require that patients in restraints be in a gown?"

"Oh. That's right." Robotically the nurse said, "we're going to have to put her in a gown."

With an unrestrained voice, the girl unleashed a primal "NO!!!!" The convulsing began again as if the tranquilizer had been adrenaline.

*This cannot be necessary,* I thought. *If she's in restraints with someone sitting here with her, how could her clothing pose a risk?*

"Can't we leave her t-shirt on?" someone offered.

The nurse thought a moment. "Melissa, I'm going to let you keep your shirt on. But we're going to sit you up, and I'm going to unsnap and slip your bra off."

In the ensuing battle I could not believe what I was seeing. Even more, I couldn't believe I was participating. The sheet would not stay over the girl. And it's whiteness made an eerie contrast to the girl's jet black t-shirt. In the top of my peripheral vision I saw her large breast briefly but completely exposed. The girl knew what I had seen as she seethed at me and screamed "F!@# YOU!!!!" She once again almost wrenched free. I pressed my finger tips more firmly into the nerve behind her earlobe. She screamed and gushed a torrent of curses at me. I looked down at her, almost crying, and whispered, "Be still. Please. It will all be over soon."

Years later when I saw the movie *Saving Private Ryan*, I couldn't sleep because of seeing one scene over and over in my mind. It was the scene where a German soldier gently shushes an American G.I. while slowly sliding a knife into his chest as the American soldier begs for mercy. As a person who grew up as the scrawny school runt, I knew I would be the one overwhelmed in such a fight. As a former psychiatric aide, I saw myself in the German soldier, shushing a terrified girl as I participated in what felt like her gang rape.

I was just following orders.

In sixth grade I read a book about the Nuremberg trials after World War II. Even as a sixth grader I thought "just following orders" was no excuse.

Now I saw the power of being swept up in the moment and being overpowered by authority. I had made the mistake once; I would not again.

As we debriefed the physical management, I voiced my objections. "She could use her bra to strangle herself," the head nurse said.

"And just how is she going to do that while drugged, and in restraints, and with someone sitting in the room with her?"

"I'm sorry, that's hospital policy."

"Well, I feel like I just took part in a gang rape. And policy or not, I will not do that again. We need to demand that policy be reviewed and changed. For crying out loud, we could have at least waited until that shot took effect and changed her after she was asleep!"

"What about that experience is so important to you now?" my counselor asked me.

"I was replaying it in my head the other day, and I realized I didn't feel guilty; I felt envious."

"Envious?"

"Yeah. I envied that that 15-year-old girl got to express her rage. I envied that she got to thrash around and scream without really hurting anybody."

"Could this be a place where you could express your rage?"

I looked at my counselor and sarcastically said, "You got about 30 cc's of Haloperidol?"

She shook her head.

At our next session she asked me where I wanted to start. I told her I needed to get some anger off my chest.

"About what?" she asked.

"About you."

She nodded for me to proceed.

"I left here really angry last week. Ironically, it was because you asked me if this could be a place where I could express my rage." I waited for her to ask the obvious question.

"What about that bothered you?"

"If I had expressed my rage in here last week, I would have picked this chair up and thrown it through that window."

My counselor again raised her eyes in apparent surprise. "Wow. I obviously was having a disconnect." She paused, searching for words. "What... did my suggestion mean to you?"

"I felt like a weakling. When I was a kid, I was such a runt. I learned to compensate by being intimidating with my eyes and intellect. With my eyes and my words I tried to communicate that I was an atom you didn't want to split. For you to invite me to express my rage in here meant you don't feel intimidated by my rage. And for you— as a petite female of all things— not to feel intimidated by my rage, then I must appear pretty weak."

She nodded with realization. "I'm glad you're telling me this. We've talked about how gender and age differences might come to play in here." (She was nine years younger than I. "You were still in college when I started my Ph.D. program," I had said one day. She continued, addressing gender stereotypes. "When I heard you say 'rage' I was thinking of an emotional and verbal response. You were talking about something physical. You obviously could do some damage," she said, gesturing to the full length of my 6'2" frame. "So what do we do about this?"

I sighed in agony and lashed out with sarcasm. "Do you have 30 cc's of Haloperidol?"

She shook her head with a look of empathy and a hint of smirk at the ridiculousness of my suggestion. Wisely, she let silence speak.

A few days later, I would be sitting in the office of one of my mentors. She was the professor with whom I had taken most of my courses, family therapy in particular. I told her I was struggling as a client. She smiled. "We're therapists, Brad. We make the worst clients. But I've never doubted your abilities. You're going to do fine." I was amazed. Dr.

Priscilla Blanton had just included *me* in the first person plural pronoun when she said *we* were therapists. And, yes, we therapists make the worst clients, because, knowing all the tricks, it's hard not to get into a chess match.

There I had sat in my counselor's office— her tastefully appointed office that accentuated the Spartan paint-peeling, plaster-falling squalor of mine; she was working as a counselor; I was grading bad papers. There I sat making my counselor play therapeutic chess with me. I thought about my counselor's question regarding what we were to do about expressing my anger. It was my move. I needed to start dealing with my rage regarding relationships outside of therapy by learning from my relationship with my therapist. I needed to be honest.

"I'm jealous of you. First of all, you're working in this great office while I'm over in what we call the Attic Dungeon with plaster falling off the ceiling and walls. You're working in this great office in the counseling program I tried to get into— but got rejected by— three times." My counselor looked shocked. "Yeah, I got rejected three times. After the third time I got rejected, I met with the department chair and asked him why— with my grades, admissions scores, and recommendations— why I wasn't being accepted. He asked me what I wanted to do. I told him I wanted to be a counselor. He laughed out loud. 'That's the problem,' he said. 'Counselors come a dime a dozen; we're looking for researchers.' Second of all, I'm jealous because you seem to have made it this far without falling apart. And, I find myself being jealous of you because you're a doing better as my counselor than I would be doing with someone like me. You're a better counselor at age 30 than I am at 39, and I'm jealous."

She nodded, wrinkled her nose, and gestured around the room. "This is a pretty nice room. Isn't it... *normal* to want something like this?"

I took the fact that she ignored the issue of her superior skills as an indication that the idea didn't even merit comment, and that felt good. Then my brain started to parse the word normal. But my thoughts were held captive by the marvelously liberating feeling of my counselor affirming my being normal.

She was nine years younger than I. But she spoke as one with authority, authority made complete by caution and compassion.

**Questions for Reflection**

1) After telling a class the story of contributing to the assault on the young woman in the psychiatric hospital, I made this comment: "After that experience I decided I would rather be the last person to follow a good order than the first one to follow a bad one." (A supervisor once told me if I wanted to advance in the organization I needed to do a better job of following orders— that I needed to see the organization like a military hierarchy. I told the supervisor I would always follow an ethical order— with the implication about the history of orders I'd received fully intended.) How would my comment about being last versus first, if followed, be risky in the military? What differences may exist between a nation's military and other organizations? What is the US military's rule about following illegal or unethical orders?

2) What is the difference between confidence and arrogance? What does that have to do with the theme of this chapter?

# EPILOGUE

Please see the "prepilogue," and consider the importance I place on the "parent" cap. Thinking of that prompts one last anecdote.

When I was working on my Ph.D., I worked as a teacher's assistant in the university's preschool. Before going into the program, I promised my wife that I would spend 30 minutes a day with each of our children and another 30 minutes at dinner each evening. About three weeks into the program, a supervisor asked me why I had not turned in paperwork in two weeks. I said, "You only give me one hour a week outside the classroom, and I can't get all the paperwork done in one hour." My supervisor said, "Well, you know, Brad, sometimes we have to do work at home." I said, "I do work at home." She— a single person with no children and who worked 80 hours a week— looked surprised and asked, "What do you do at home?" Matter-of-factly, I said, "I raise my children." I let that sink in and continued: "I left a good job with a well-appointed office and two secretaries in order to come back to school. I am taking a double full-time course load. I work another part-time job. I have a signed contract for a 20-hour a week graduate assistantship. If you will decide how you want me to spend those hours, I will give you 20 excellent hours a week; not 19:45 and not 20:15. Twenty."

The next week I had two hours of prep time outside the classroom. Years later, when I lost my teaching job to budget cuts, I told my children: "I don't know how long it will take me to find another job. We don't have a fancy house or cable TV, but we may have to be even more frugal; we may have to give up our cell phones and things like that." My then 10-year-old son said, "Dad, I don't have to buy those magnets I wanted, you can have my $5. Will that help?" I believe the risk I took defending my parent-cap was worth the pricelessness of that offer.

CPSIA information can be obtained
at www.ICGtesting.com
Printed in the USA
LVOW07s0609231017
553421LV00025B/304/P